Discover You

Career Guide for Students, Parents & Educators Powered by AI

Authors: Logesh Arumugam, Giri K S

Co-Authors: SG Srevatshen, Ritvik L

Copyright © 2025 Logesh Arumugam & Giri K S

Made with ❤ on the Notion Press Platform

www.notionpress.com

With gratitude to the Universe, for being the inspiration behind every discovery and creation.

Contents

Disclaimer

This book is intended to provide general guidance and information on knowing about various careers, and related topics. The content reflects the author's personal insights, experiences, and research, and is meant for informational and educational purposes only. While every effort has been made to ensure the accuracy and reliability of the information provided, the author and publisher assume no responsibility for errors, omissions, or outcomes resulting from the application of the content in this book. Readers are encouraged to seek professional advice tailored to their specific circumstances before making career-related decisions. The book does not guarantee employment, promotions, or specific results and should not be considered as a substitute for professional career counseling. Any reliance on the information provided in this book is solely at the reader's discretion. The author and publisher disclaim any liability for any losses or damages incurred as a result of using or misusing the information contained in this book.

About Authors & Co-Authors

Logesh Arumugam	https://www.linkedin.com/in/logesh-arumugam-67aa845/
Giri K S	https://www.linkedin.com/in/giri-ks-98a89533/
SG Srevatshen	https://www.linkedin.com/in/srevatshen-s-g-220b87277/
Ritvik L	https://www.linkedin.com/in/ritvik-l-bb5678234/

Introduction

Discover You is an outcome of a detailed study on global occupations that is classified into more than 400-unit groups [**ref. ISCO & NCO**]. We have chosen carefully 90 careers intending to create or bring awareness to younger generation, parents and educators.

"Discover You" serves as the ultimate guide for students, delving into **90 exciting career paths**, while empowering parents to support diverse opportunities and equipping educators to guide students on their journey of self-discovery. Featuring **references to over 900 companies, institutes and organizations**. The book provides a comprehensive resource, including detailed insights into various **emerging careers in AI.**

Featuring a QR code, it provides instant access to engaging, **AI-powered career videos** tailored for students, parents, and educators. Additionally, it includes sample prompts for ChatGPT, Microsoft Co-Pilot, Google Gemini, DeepSeek enabling readers to dive deeper into limitless possibilities and gain valuable insights to confidently shape their future.

The comprehensive **list of career journey tracks** ensures that every reader has a clear and actionable roadmap tailored to their unique interests and potential.

Discover You also covers **key Behavioural skills / Soft Skills** students should focus on during early days which is essential for personal growth, building relationships, and preparing for future challenges.

<u>About ISCO & NCO:</u>

ISCO stands for **International Standard Classification of Occupations**, a system developed by the **International Labour Organization (ILO)** to categorize and organize different occupations systematically. ISCO provides a framework for:

1. **Classifying Jobs:** It groups jobs into standardized categories based on tasks and skill levels.

2. **Comparing Data:** Facilitates international comparisons of occupational data, including employment statistics.

3. **Policy Development:** Supports education, training, and labour market policies by identifying skill requirements.

The **National Classification of Occupations (NCO)** is a standardized system used to classify and organize job roles in a country. It is designed to align with international systems like the **International Standard Classification of Occupations (ISCO)** to ensure consistency and comparability of occupational data.

This system is widely used by governments, researchers, and organizations for workforce planning, skills analysis, and labour market studies.

Chapter 1: Ways to "Discover You" in 90 Days!

Use the following steps to Discover You in 90 days.

Day 1:

❑ **Step 1: Know the Career:** Go through the details about the career from "Discover You" book e.g., Aeronautical Engineer – Duration: Approx. 5 Minutes

    ❑ About Aeronautical Engineer

    ❑ Where you can work if you become an Aeronautical Engineer – Go through the list from the book

Refer: Chapter 3 [1 to 90 careers]

❑ **Step 2: Watch the Video:** Scan the QR code and go through the respective video in "Discover You" YouTube channel. https://www.youtube.com/@DiscoverYou-09 e.g., Aeronautical Engineer - Duration: Approx. 5 Minutes

Refer: Chapter 2

❏ **Step 3: Visit Website of Companies:** Go through Few Companies listed from the Book and see their website e.g. In Aeronautical Engineer career – go to website of Boeing, Airbus – Duration: Approx. 10 Minutes

Refer: Chapter 3 [1 to 90 careers – Where you can work section]

❏ **Step 4: Using Prompts:** Ask relevant Questions to Chat GPT / Microsoft Co-pilot / Google Gemini related to particular career. Duration: 30 Minutes

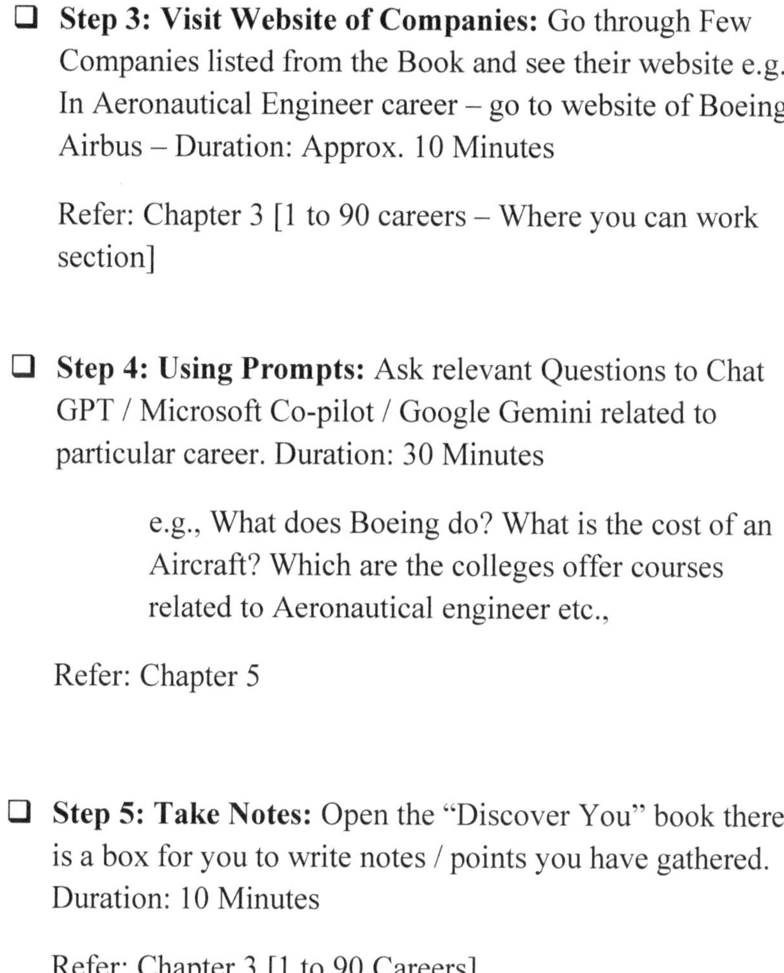

e.g., What does Boeing do? What is the cost of an Aircraft? Which are the colleges offer courses related to Aeronautical engineer etc.,

Refer: Chapter 5

❏ **Step 5: Take Notes:** Open the "Discover You" book there is a box for you to write notes / points you have gathered. Duration: 10 Minutes

Refer: Chapter 3 [1 to 90 Careers]

Note: *Additionally refer Chapter 4 for Emerging New Careers in AI, Chapter 6 to know about Career Journey Tracks and Chapter 7 for Behavioural / Soft Skills.*

Stick to this for 90 days, and you'll unlock your true potential, paving the way for confident and career-defining decisions!

Chapter 2: "Discover You" YouTube Channel

Step 1: Scan the above QR code from your mobile

Step 2: Automatically opens YouTube "Discover You" Channel – https://www.youtube.com/@DiscoverYou-09

Step 3: Navigate and Search for the video you are looking to know about a particular career

Note: Videos are generated by AI software.

Chapter 3: Discover You

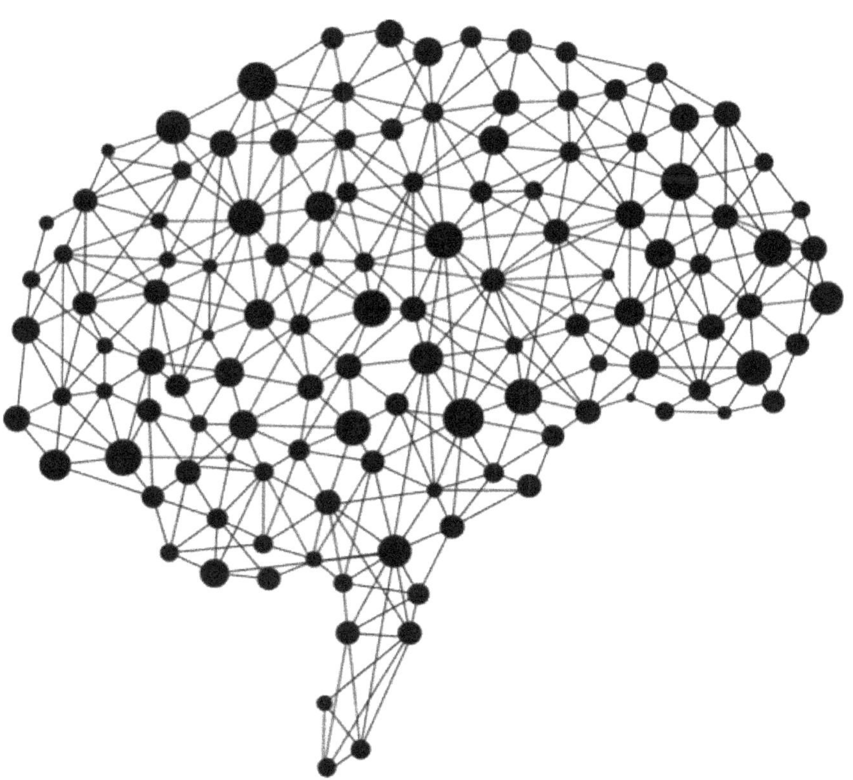

Learn Until Your Signature becomes Autograph!

1. Aeronautical Engineer

An Aeronautical Engineer specializes in the design, development, testing, and production of aircraft and related systems. They focus on improving flight technology, ensuring safety, efficiency, and performance in both commercial and military aviation.

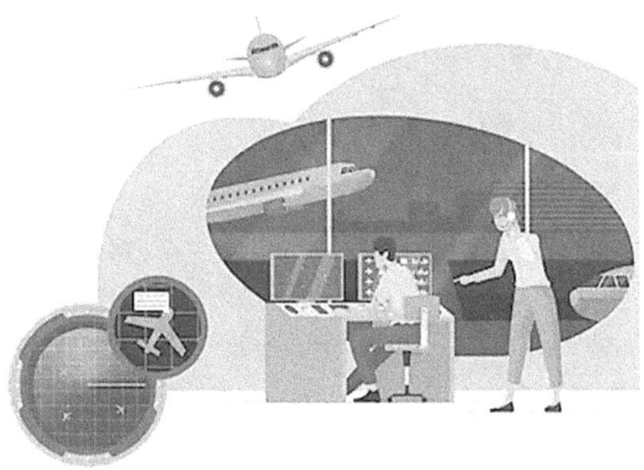

"Aeronautical engineers are the architects of the sky"

Where you can work: Boeing, Airbus, Lockheed Martin, Northrop, Grumman, Raytheon Technologies, General Electric Aviation, Rolls-Royce, SpaceX, NASA, BAE Systems, Safran, Embraer, Bombardier, Dassault Aviation, Thales Group

2. Animator

An Animator creates moving images by designing and sequencing a series of frames, bringing characters, scenes, and stories to life. They use artistic skills and software tools to produce animations for films, video games, advertisements, and digital media.

"An Animator breathes life into imagination, turning still images into stories that move and inspire."

Where you can work: Pixer Animation Studios, Walt Disney Animation Studios, DreamWorks Animation, Sony Pictures Animation, Blue Sky Studios, Nickelodeon Animation Studio, Cartoon Network Studios, Warner Bros. Animation, Ubisoft, Netflix Animation

3. Architect

An architect designs and plans buildings, structures, aesthetics, and safety to create spaces that meet client needs comply with regulations. They oversee projects from concept to completion, ensuring that designs are both innovative and structurally sound.

"An architect turns dreams into spaces, crafting the blueprint of tomorrow with creativity and precision."

Where you can work: Larsen & Toubro (L&T), Tata Projects, Shapoorji Pallonji, Hindustan Construction Company (HCC), Gammon India, Sobha Developers, DLF, GMR Group, AFCONS Infrastructure, Reliance Infrastructure

4. Auditor

An auditor examines financial records and processes to ensure accuracy, compliance with regulations, and the integrity of financial reporting. They provide insights and recommendations for improving financial practices and safeguarding against fraud or errors.

"An auditor is the guardian of financial truth, ensuring every number tells the right story."

Where you can work: Deloitte, PricewaterhouseCoopers (PwC), Ernst & Young (EY), KPMG, JP Morgan Chase, Goldman Sachs, Citibank, HSBC, Wells Fargo, Accounting firms, government agencies, financial institutions, corporate finance departments, non-profit organizations, and internal audit departments of various companies and also as independent consultants

5. Automotive Engineer

An automotive engineer designs, develops, and tests vehicles and their components, focusing on performance, safety, and efficiency. They work on everything from engines and transmissions to electrical systems and aerodynamics, ensuring that vehicles meet industry standards and consumer needs.

"Turning vision into vehicles, an automotive engineer blends technology and creativity to redefine mobility."

Where you can work: Tesla, Ford Motor Company, General Motors (GM), BMW Group, Mercedes-Benz, Toyota, Honda, Volkswagen Group, Nissan, Hyundai Motor Company

6. Ayurveda Doctor

An Ayurveda doctor practices traditional Indian medicine, focusing on natural remedies and holistic approaches to maintain health and treat illness. They use a combination of herbal treatments, dietary guidelines, and lifestyle changes to balance the body's energies and promote overall well-being.

""Nature's cure, crafted by an Ayurveda doctor."

Where you can work: Patanjali Ayurveda, Himalaya Wellness, Dabur India, Baidyanath, Arya Vaidya Sala, Zandu Pharmaceuticals, Kottakkal Arya Vaidya Sala, Jiva Ayurveda, Kerala Ayurveda, Vedicure Healthcare

7. Bio Medical Engineer

A biomedical engineer designs and develops medical devices, equipment, and software to improve patient care and healthcare delivery. They blend principles of engineering with medical sciences to create innovative solutions for diagnosing, monitoring, and treating medical conditions.

"Merging engineering with medicine, biomedical engineers enhance lives through innovation."

Where you can work: Medtronic, Siemens, Philips Healthcare, GE Healthcare, Baxter International, Boston Scientific, Johnson & Johnson, Stryker, Abbott Laboratories, Thermo Fisher Scientific

8. Bio Technologist

A biotechnologist applies biological principles and techniques to develop products and processes in various fields such as medicine, agriculture, and environmental management. They work on creating innovations like genetic modifications, biopharmaceuticals, and sustainable solutions to address complex biological challenges.

"Biotechnologists harness the power of biology to drive innovation and transform life sciences."

Where you can work: Genentech, Amgen, Biogen, Roche, Gilead Sciences, Illumina, Novozymes, Syngenta, Monsanto, Thermo Fisher Scientific

9. Broadcast Engineer

A broadcast engineer manages and operates the technical equipment used in radio, television, and online media broadcasting. They ensure the smooth transmission of content by maintaining equipment, troubleshooting issues, and overseeing signal quality and broadcast standards.

"Broadcast engineers are the silent architects behind the airwaves, ensuring every signal reaches its audience seamlessly."

Where you can work: BBC (British Broadcasting Corporation), CNN, NBCUniversal, Disney-ABC Television Group, Sky Group, Fox Broadcasting Company, CBS Corporation, ESPN, ViacomCBS, All India Radio, TATA Sky, Doordarshan

10. Career Counselor

A career counselor helps individuals identify their strengths, interests, and career goals, providing guidance on education, job opportunities, and professional development. They offer personalized advice and support, helping clients make informed decisions about their career paths and navigate the job market.

"A career counselor illuminates the path to your future, guiding you toward your true potential."

Where you can work: Educational Testing Service (ETS), LinkedIn, Indeed, Kaplan, CollegeBoard, Pearson Education, The Princeton Review, Randstad, Adecco, CareerBuilder

11. Ceramic Engineer

A ceramic engineer focuses on the research, design, and production of ceramic materials, which are crucial for applications in industries like electronics, aerospace, and construction. They work to enhance the performance of ceramics, ensuring these materials meet specific technical requirements such as strength, thermal resistance, and electrical insulation.

"From pottery to spacecraft, ceramic engineers build the unbreakable foundations of innovation."

Where you can work: Kajaria Ceramics, Somany Ceramics, Cera Sanitaryware, Nitco Limited, Asian Granito India Limited, RAK Ceramics India, Johnson Tiles, Hindustan Ceramic Industries, Simpolo Ceramic, Tata Ceramics

12. Chef

A chef is a professional who plans and prepares meals, oversees kitchen operations, and ensures the quality and presentation of dishes. They use their culinary expertise to create diverse and flavorful dishes, manage kitchen staff, and maintain a clean and efficient cooking environment.

"Crafting Culinary Magic, One Dish at a Time."

Where you can work: Taj Hotels, Oberoi Hotels & Resorts, ITC Hotels, Leela Palaces, Marriott Hotels, Hyatt Hotels, Radisson Blu Hotels, Accor Group, Hilton Hotels, Catering companies, Private dining establishments, Food and beverage startups, corporate dining services, Culinary schools, Food networks, Cloud Kitchens

13. Chemist

A chemist studies and manipulates the composition, structure, and properties of substances to develop new materials, products, and processes. They conduct experiments and analyze chemical reactions to solve problems and create innovative solutions in industries ranging from pharmaceuticals to manufacturing.

"From lab to life, a chemist's work is the catalyst for discovery and progress."

Where you can work: Dr. Reddy's Laboratories, Cipla, Sun Pharmaceutical Industries, Glenmark Pharmaceuticals, Lupin Limited, Aurobindo Pharma, Biocon, Zydus Cadila, Mylan Laboratories, Torrent Pharmaceuticals

14. Cinematographer

A cinematographer, also known as a director of photography, is responsible for capturing the visual essence of a film or television production through camera work and lighting. They work closely with directors to create the visual style and mood of the project, ensuring that each scene effectively conveys the intended story and emotion.

"A cinematographer paints with light and shadow, bringing stories to life through the lens of creativity."

Where you can work: Warner Bros., Universal Pictures, Paramount Pictures, Sony Pictures, 20th Century Studios, Netflix, HBO, Amazon Studios, Lionsgate, MGM Studios

15. Civil Engineer

A Civil Engineer designs, plans, and oversees the construction and maintenance of infrastructure projects like roads, bridges, buildings, and water systems. They ensure the safety, functionality, and sustainability of structures, contributing to the development of communities and cities.

"Civil engineers build the foundation for a sustainable future, turning blueprints into the structures that shape our world."

Where you can work: Larsen & Toubro (L&T), Tata Projects, Shapoorji Pallonji, Hindustan Construction Company (HCC), Gammon India, Sobha Developers, DLF, GMR Group, AFCONS Infrastructure, Reliance Infrastructure

16. Clinical Researcher

A Clinical Researcher designs, conducts, and analyzes clinical trials to test the safety and efficacy of medical treatments, drugs, and devices. They play a crucial role in advancing medical knowledge by adhering to ethical guidelines and regulatory standards while ensuring the well-being of study participants.

"Advancing medicine through research, with precision and care for humanity."

Where you can work: Pfizer, Novartis, Roche, Johnson & Johnson, GlaxoSmithKline (GSK), Merck & Co., Sanofi, AstraZeneca, Parexel, ICON plc

17. Clothing & Textile Technologist

A Clothing and Textile Technologist works on the design, development, production of fabrics, garments ensuring quality, durability, and functionality. They test materials, research new textiles, and optimize production processes to meet industry standards and consumer demands.

"Crafting the future of fashion through innovation and fabric expertise."

Where you can work: Arvind Mills, Raymond, Welspun India, Vardhman Textiles, Aditya Birla Fashion and Retail, Reliance Industries (Textile Division), Page Industries, Trident Group, Grasim Industries, Bombay Dyeing

18. Cloud Computing Specialist

A Cloud Computing Specialist is an IT professional responsible for designing, managing, and maintaining cloud infrastructure and services. They ensure seamless data storage, processing, and security using platforms like AWS, Azure, or Google Cloud, optimizing performance and cost-efficiency for organizations.

"Optimizing today's infrastructure for tomorrow's digital challenges with cloud expertise."

Where you can work: Amazon Web Services (AWS), Microsoft Azure, Google Cloud Platform (GCP), IBM Cloud, Oracle Cloud, Salesforce, VMware, Rackspace, Cisco Systems

19. Criminologist

A criminologist studies crime, criminal behavior, and the societal responses to crime, using theories and research methods from sociology, psychology, and law. They analyze crime patterns, develop crime prevention strategies, and contribute to the understanding of the criminal justice system to inform policy and practice.

"Understanding crime is the first step towards creating a safer society."

Where you can work: NIA, RAW, CBI, ED, Federal Bureau of Investigation (FBI), Department of Justice, Bureau of Alcohol, Tobacco, Firearms and Explosives (ATF), Police Departments, National Crime Agency (NCA), Criminal Justice Research Institutes, Private Security Firms, Universities and Colleges (as educators or researchers), Consulting Firms (e.g., Deloitte, McKinsey & Company)

20. Cyber Security Specialist

A Cyber Security Specialist is an expert in protecting computer systems, networks, and data from cyber threats and attacks. They implement security measures, monitor for vulnerabilities, and respond to incidents to ensure the safety and integrity of digital assets

"Cyber Security Specialists are the guardians of the digital world, tirelessly defending against unseen threats to keep our data safe and secure."

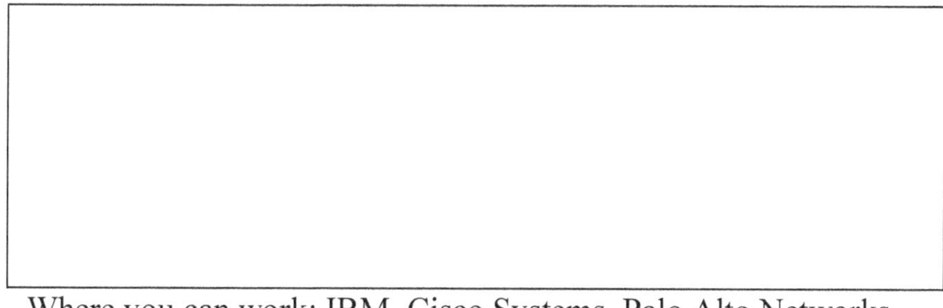

Where you can work: IBM, Cisco Systems, Palo Alto Networks, McAfee, Symantec (NortonLifeLock), FireEye, CrowdStrike, Deloitte, KPMG, PwC, EY (Ernst & Young), RSA Security

21. Data Analyst

A Data Analyst is a professional who collects, processes, and analyzes data to uncover insights and support decision-making within an organization. They utilize statistical tools and data visualization techniques to interpret trends and patterns, helping to drive strategic business initiatives.

"Data is the new oil; it fuels informed decisions and drives innovation."

Where you can work: Google, Microsoft, Amazon, Facebook (Meta), Apple, IBM, Deloitte, Accenture, PwC, KPMG, EY (Ernst & Young), McKinsey & Company, Nielsen

22. Data Visualization Expert

A Data Visualization Expert specializes in transforming complex data sets into clear and engaging visual representations, making information more accessible and understandable. They use tools and techniques to create charts, graphs, and dashboards that help stakeholders make informed decisions based on data-driven insights.

"Data visualization is not just about presenting information; it's about telling a story that drives understanding and action."

Where you can work: Tableau, Microsoft, Qlik, Google, IBM, SAP, SAS, Oracle, All Software companies where Visualization expertise is required

23. Data Scientist

A Data Scientist is a professional who uses statistical analysis, machine learning, and data visualization techniques to extract insights from complex datasets and drive decision-making. They bridge the gap between data and actionable strategies for businesses.

"A Data Scientist is a storyteller with data as their language."

Where you can work: Google, Amazon, Microsoft, Facebook (Meta), IBM, Apple, Netflix, LinkedIn, Airbnb, Salesforce, Twitter, Uber, Adobe, Tesla, NVIDIA

24. Database Administrator

A Database Administrator (DBA) is responsible for the installation, configuration, maintenance, and security of databases, ensuring their performance and availability for users. They manage data storage, backup, recovery, and implement policies to maintain data integrity and security while optimizing database performance.

"Every byte matter; a Database Administrator ensures that data flows smoothly and securely."

Where you can work: Oracle, Microsoft, IBM, Amazon Web Services (AWS), Google, SAP, Dell Technologies, Cisco Systems, Accenture, Capgemini, Infosys, Tata Consultancy Services (TCS), HCL Technologies, Wipro, NetSuite (a subsidiary of Oracle)

25. Dentist

A Dentist specializes in diagnosing, treating, and preventing oral health issues, including diseases of the teeth, gums, and other related structures. They perform procedures such as fillings, extractions, and root canals, while also educating patients on proper dental hygiene and care.

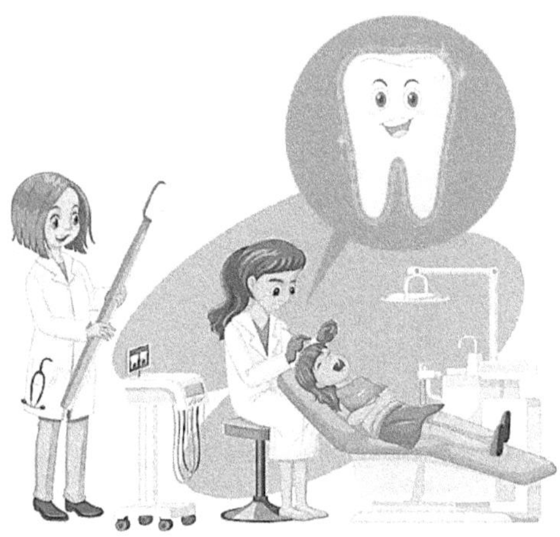

"Behind every great smile is a Dentist who cared enough to make it shine."

Where you can work: Aspen Dental, Heartland Dental, DentalOne Partners, Pacific Dental Services, Kool Smiles, Smile Brands, Apollo Dental, Dental Research Centers, Any Dental Hospitals, Independent Clinic

26. Dermatologist

A dermatologist is a medical professional specializing in the diagnosis and treatment of skin, hair, and nail disorders. They address a wide range of conditions, from acne and eczema to skin cancers and cosmetic concerns, using both medical and surgical techniques.

"Healthy skin is a reflection of overall wellness; let a dermatologist guide your journey to radiant beauty."

Where you can work: All India Institute of Medical Sciences (AIIMS), Christian Medical College (CMC), Apollo Hospitals, Fortis Healthcare, Manipal Hospitals, Dermatology Clinics, Cosmetic Surgery Centers, Pharmaceutical Companies, Research Institutions, Skincare Product Manufacturers, Telemedicine Health Insurance Companies, Medical Colleges

27. Design Engineer

A design engineer is responsible for creating and developing innovative designs for products or systems, utilizing engineering principles and software tools. They collaborate with cross-functional teams to ensure functionality, manufacturability, and cost-effectiveness while adhering to industry standards and regulations.

"Design engineers turn ideas into reality, crafting solutions that shape the future."

Where you can work: Aerospace Companies, Automotive Manufacturers, Electronics Firms, Consumer Goods Companies, Construction and Engineering Firms, Industrial Design Consultancies, Software Development Companies, Defense Contractors, Renewable Energy Companies, Research and Development Organizations

28. Dietitian

A dietitian is a healthcare professional who specializes in nutrition, helping individuals develop healthy eating habits and personalized meal plans based on their medical needs and lifestyle. They work to prevent and manage diseases by promoting balanced diets and fostering overall wellness.

"Eat for the body you want, not just the taste you crave."

Where you can work: Hospitals and Clinics, Fitness Centers and Gyms, Corporate Wellness Programs, Food and Beverage Companies (e.g., Nestlé, PepsiCo), Public Health Organizations (e.g., WHO, UNICEF), Research Institutions (e.g., National Institutes of Health), Health and Wellness Startups, Educational Institutions, Sports Teams and Athletic Organizations, Government Health Departments

29. Doctor

A doctor is a compassionate healer dedicated to diagnosing, treating, and caring for patients to improve their health and quality of life. With a blend of medical expertise and empathy, they strive to bring comfort, hope, and healing to those in need.

"A doctor's purpose is not just to treat, but to care and understand."

Where you can work: Apollo Hospitals, Fortis Healthcare, Mayo Clinic, Cleveland Clinic, Max Healthcare, NHS (National Health Service), Johns Hopkins Medicine, HCA Healthcare, Kaiser Permanente, Medanta, WHO (World Health Organization), UNICEF, Indian Health Service (IHS), Mount Sinai Health System

30. Economist

An economist studies how resources are produced, distributed, and consumed, analyzing trends to understand and predict economic behavior. They provide insights and solutions to complex financial issues, helping shape policies and strategies for sustainable economic growth.

"Guided by data, economists illuminate the path to a balanced and thriving economy."

Where you can work: World Bank, International Monetary Fund (IMF), Federal Reserve Bank, United Nations (UN), OECD (Organization for Economic Co-operation and Development), McKinsey & Company, Boston Consulting Group (BCG), Deloitte, Goldman Sachs, PwC (PricewaterhouseCoopers), Citibank, Bank of England, National Bureau of Economic Research (NBER), Brookings Institution, Economic Policy Institute (EPI)

31. Electrical Engineer

An electrical engineer designs, develops, and maintains electrical systems and equipment, applying principles of electricity, electronics, and electromagnetism. They work across various industries, creating solutions that enhance efficiency, safety, and sustainability in power generation, transmission, and electronic systems.

"Electrical engineers power the future, transforming ideas into electrifying realities."

Where you can work: Siemens, General Electric (GE), Schneider Electric, ABB, Honeywell, Siemens Energy, Eaton, Texas Instruments, Raytheon Technologies, Lockheed Martin, Northrop Grumman, Emerson Electric, Mitsubishi Electric, Philips, Rockwell Automation

32. Electronics Engineer

An electronic engineer designs and develops electronic circuits, devices, and systems, focusing on innovation in telecommunications, robotics, and consumer electronics. They combine principles of physics and mathematics to create solutions that enhance technology and improve everyday life.

"Electronic engineers transform circuits into solutions, shaping the way we communicate and interact."

Where you can work: Intel, Texas Instruments, Qualcomm, Nvidia, Broadcom, Samsung Electronics, Sony, Bosch, Analog Devices, National Instruments, Philips, Motorola Solutions, Honeywell, Cirrus Logic, ON Semiconductor

33. Embedded Programmer

An embedded engineer specializes in designing and developing embedded systems, which are computer systems integrated into larger devices to perform specific functions. They combine hardware and software expertise to create efficient, reliable solutions for applications in industries such as automotive, consumer electronics, and industrial automation.

"Embedded engineers bring intelligence to everyday devices, seamlessly integrating technology into our lives."

Where you can work: Intel, Nvidia, Qualcomm, Texas Instruments, NXP Semiconductors, STMicroelectronics, Microchip Technology, Analog Devices, Bosch, Renesas Electronics, Cypress Semiconductor, Broadcom, ARM Holdings, Huawei, Samsung Electronics, IBM

34. Ethical Hacker

An ethical hacker uses their skills to identify and address vulnerabilities in computer systems, networks, and applications, ensuring security and protection against malicious attacks. By simulating cyber threats, they help organizations safeguard their data and maintain robust defenses in an increasingly digital world.

"In the world of cybersecurity, ethical hackers are the unsung heroes, defending against unseen dangers."

Where you can work: IBM, Cisco Systems, Palo Alto Networks, FireEye, Check Point Software Technologies, McAfee, Symantec, CrowdStrike, Rapid7, Deloitte, Accenture, Booz Allen Hamilton, Kaspersky Lab, Trend Micro, Verizon Cyber Risk Solutions

35. Fashion Designer

A fashion designer creates innovative clothing, accessories, and footwear, blending creativity with functionality to express individual style and cultural trends. They analyze market demands and fabric technologies to develop unique collections that captivate and inspire consumers.

"Fashion designers transform fabric into stories, giving life to creativity and culture through every stitch."

Where you can work: Chanel, Gucci, Prada, Louis Vuitton, Versace, Calvin Klein, Ralph Lauren, Tommy Hilfiger, Burberry, Dolce & Gabbana, Nike, Adidas, H&M, Zara, Lululemon

36. Food Technologist

A food technologist specializes in the science and technology of food production, focusing on improving the safety, quality, and nutritional value of food products. They work across various sectors, including research and development, quality control, and food processing, ensuring that food meets industry standards and consumer demands.

"In every bite we take, food technologists ensure that taste meets safety and nutrition harmoniously."

Where you can work: Nestlé, PepsiCo, Britannia Industries, ITC Limited, Amul, Parle Agro, Hindustan Unilever Limited, Coca-Cola, Hatsun Agro Products, Heritage Foods, MTR Foods, Haldiram's, Everest Spices, Central Food Technological Research Institute (CFTRI), FSSAI-approved labs

37. Graphics Designer

A graphic designer creates visual content to communicate messages and ideas, utilizing typography, color, imagery, and layout to engage audiences. They work across various media, from print to digital, bringing brands to life and enhancing user experiences through innovative design solutions.

"Graphic designers turn ideas into visual stories, crafting compelling images that communicate and inspire."

Where you can work: Adobe, Apple, Google, Microsoft, IBM, Nike, Coca-Cola, Starbucks, Amazon, Facebook (Meta), Pixar, Warner Bros., National Geographic, 20th Century Fox, Viacom CBS

38. Human Resource Manager

A Human Resource officer manages recruitment, employee relations, and organizational development to support a productive and positive workplace. They bridge the gap between management and staff, ensuring compliance, fostering growth, and aligning workforce strategies with company goals.

"HR officers cultivate a culture of respect, helping individuals and organizations reach their fullest potential."

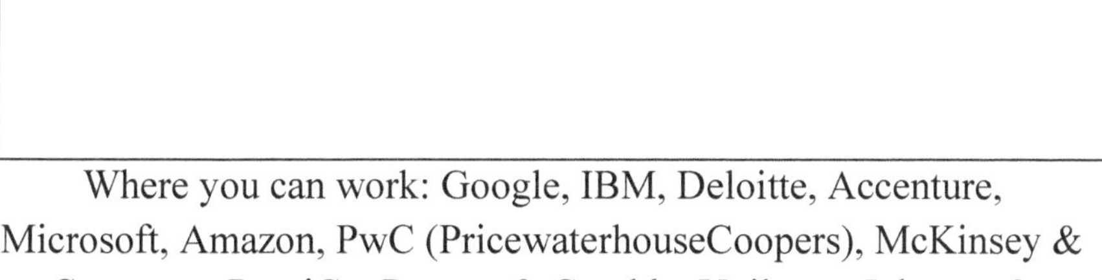

Where you can work: Google, IBM, Deloitte, Accenture, Microsoft, Amazon, PwC (PricewaterhouseCoopers), McKinsey & Company, PepsiCo, Procter & Gamble, Unilever, Johnson & Johnson, Goldman Sachs, JPMorgan Chase, Coca-Cola

39. Industrial Engineer

An Industrial Engineer officer optimizes complex systems and processes, improving efficiency, productivity, and cost-effectiveness across various industries. They analyze workflows, materials, and resources to develop solutions that enhance operational performance and quality standards.

"Industrial engineers bring precision to processes, transforming ideas into efficient and effective solutions."

Where you can work: Boeing, Ford Motor Company, General Electric (GE), Siemens, Toyota, Caterpillar Inc., Lockheed Martin, Amazon, Tesla, Intel, Procter & Gamble, 3M, Johnson & Johnson, Honeywell

40. Instrumentation Engineer

An Instrumentation Engineer specializes in designing, developing, and managing systems and devices for measuring and controlling engineering processes. They ensure accurate data acquisition and process stability, which are crucial in industries like manufacturing, energy, and automation.

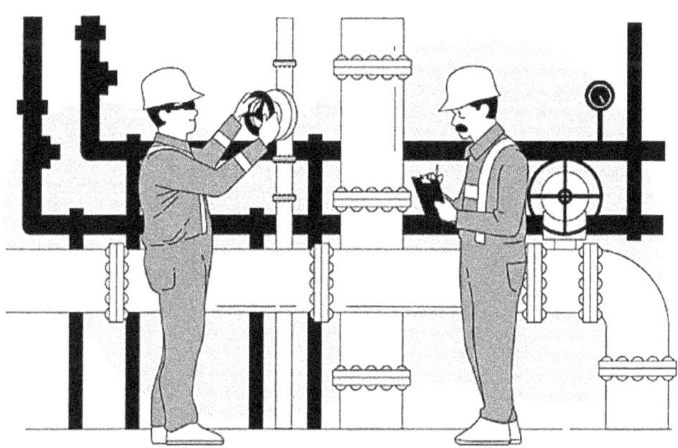

"Instrumentation engineers are the guardians of precision, ensuring every measurement drives accuracy and efficiency."

Where you can work: Siemens, ABB, Honeywell, Emerson Electric, Yokogawa Electric, General Electric (GE), Schneider Electric, Rockwell Automation, Schlumberger, Mitsubishi Electric, Baker Hughes, Bosch, Endress+Hauser, Hitachi, Larsen & Toubro (L&T)

41. Insurance Expert

An Insurance Expert offers guidance on risk management and policy selection to help individuals and businesses protect assets while mitigating financial losses.They assess needs, analyze market offerings, and develop tailored insurance solutions that provide security and peace of mind.

"Insurance experts safeguard futures, turning uncertainties into manageable risks."

Where you can work: Allianz, AIG (American International Group), Prudential Financial, State Farm, AXA, MetLife, Zurich Insurance Group, Liberty Mutual, Marsh & McLennan, Berkshire Hathaway, Manulife, Chubb, Aviva

42. Interpreter

An interpreter facilitates clear and accurate communication across language barriers, enabling effective interaction in diverse settings like business, healthcare, and diplomacy. They translate spoken words in real-time, ensuring understanding and fostering collaboration between speakers of different languages.

"Interpreters are the bridge between languages, turning words into connections."

Where you can work: United Nations, European Union, LanguageLine Solutions, TransPerfect, Lionbridge, CyraCom, Global Interpreting Network, Morningside Translations, Welocalize, National Security Agency (NSA), RWS Group, International Monetary Fund (IMF)

43. Investment Manager

An Investment Manager analyzes financial markets and assets, making strategic decisions to grow and safeguard clients' wealth. They develop customized portfolios, balancing risk and return to achieve long-term financial goals for individuals or institutions.

"Investment managers turn opportunities into growth, guiding wealth with strategy and foresight."

Where you can work: BlackRock, Vanguard Group, JPMorgan Chase, Goldman Sachs, Fidelity Investments, Morgan Stanley, UBS, Charles Schwab, State Street Global Advisors, PIMCO, T. Rowe Price, Capital Group, Wellington Management, Franklin Templeton, Northern Trust

44. IoT Specialist

An IoT Specialist focuses on designing and implementing Internet of Things (IoT) solutions that connect devices and systems to collect and analyze data, enhancing automation and efficiency. They work across various industries to develop innovative applications that leverage real-time data for improved decision-making and operational effectiveness.

"IoT specialists turn everyday objects into smart solutions, revolutionizing how we interact with technology."

Where you can work: Cisco Systems, IBM, Microsoft, Amazon Web Services (AWS), Google, Siemens, GE Digital, Intel, PTC, Bosch, Honeywell, Oracle, SAP, Accenture, Dell Technologies

45. Journalist

A journalist investigates, reports, and writes news stories, providing accurate and timely information to the public on various topics, including politics, culture, and current events. They play a crucial role in shaping public opinion and holding institutions accountable through their commitment to truth and ethical reporting.

"Journalists illuminate the truth, giving voice to the voiceless and shaping the narrative of our times."

Where you can work: The Times of India, Hindustan Times, The Hindu, Indian Express, Deccan Chronicle, NDTV, CNN-News18, India Today, Reuters India, BBC News, CNN, Reuters, Associated Press (AP), All India Radio, The Guardian, Bloomberg, Politico, Time Magazine, Forbes, Vox Media, The Washington Post, News Channels

46. Landscape Architect

A Landscape Architect designs outdoor spaces, integrating natural and built environments to create aesthetically pleasing and functional landscapes. They consider factors such as ecology, sustainability, and cultural context to enhance the beauty and utility of parks, gardens, and urban areas.

"Landscape architects sculpt the earth, transforming visions into vibrant spaces where nature and design coexist."

Where you can work: Real Estate and Construction Companies - DLF, Godrej Properties, Tata Housing. Ministry of Housing & Urban Development. Architect & Design Firms. Environmental & Sustainability Organizations - Ecological Society, CSE (Centre for Science & Environment). School of Planning & Architecture. L&T, GMR group, Archaeological Survey of India (ASI), Independent Consultants etc.,

47. Lawyer

A lawyer provides legal advice and representation to clients, navigating complex legal issues and advocating for their rights in various settings, including courts and negotiations. They specialize in different areas of law, such as criminal, corporate, family, or environmental law, ensuring justice and compliance with the legal system.

"Lawyers are the defenders of justice, wielding the law as a shield for the vulnerable and a sword for the righteous."

Where you can work: Bar Associations, Law Firms, Corporate Law departments, NGO's, Legal Aid Services, National Judicial Academy, National Law Universities, Public Service Undertakings (PSUs). And Companies like - ICICI Bank, HDFC Bank, Tata Group, Reliance Industries, Aditya Birla Group, Self Practice

48. Leather Technologist

A leather technologist specializes in the science and technology of leather production, processing, and quality control, ensuring that leather products meet industry standards and consumer demands. They work on the entire leather manufacturing process, from raw material selection to finished goods, focusing on sustainability and innovation in leather applications.

"Leather technologists craft excellence, transforming raw hides into timeless creations through skill and innovation."

Where you can work: Bata India Limited, Superhouse Group, Tanning and Leather Research Institute (TLRI), Leela Tanning Company, Liberty Shoes Limited, Puma, Adidas, Shoe Express, Chambal Fertilisers and Chemicals Limited, Ravindra Leather, Reliance Industries Limited, Hidesign, National Institute of Fashion Technology (NIFT)

49. Lecturer

A lecturer imparts knowledge and facilitates learning in academic institutions, specializing in specific subjects at the undergraduate or postgraduate level. They engage students through lectures, discussions, and assessments while contributing to curriculum development and academic research.

"Lecturers shape minds and inspire futures, illuminating the path of knowledge with passion and dedication."

Where you can work: Universities, Colleges, National Institutes of Technology (NITs), Indian Institutes of Management (IIMs), Indian School of Business (ISB), National Law Universities (NLUs), Vocational Training Institutes (e.g., National Skill Development Corporation), Online Education Platforms (e.g., Coursera, Udemy, edX), Distance Education Institutes, Research Institutes, Private Coaching Centers, International Schools and Colleges

50. Legal Advisor

A legal advisor provides expert legal counsel to individuals, businesses, or organizations, ensuring compliance with laws and regulations while mitigating risks associated with legal issues. They draft and review contracts, offer strategic advice, and represent clients in negotiations or disputes to protect their interests.

"Legal advisors are the navigators of the law, guiding clients through complex legal waters with expertise and integrity."

Where you can work: Corporate Law Firms, Multinational Corporations, Financial Institutions, Government Agencies, Non-Governmental Organizations (NGOs), Public Sector Undertakings (PSUs), Startups, Insurance Companies, Real Estate Firms, Educational Institutions, Consulting Firms, Trade Organizations, Tech Companies like Infosys, Wipro, HCL, TCS etc.,

51. Marine Engineer

A marine engineer designs, builds, and maintains systems and equipment for marine vessels and offshore structures, focusing on safety, efficiency, and environmental compliance.They work on various aspects of ship construction, propulsion, and onboard systems, contributing to the advancement of maritime technology.

"Marine engineers are the architects of the sea, powering the vessels that navigate our oceans and ensuring their journeys are safe and sustainable."

Where you can work: Cochin Shipyard Limited, Mazagon Dock Shipbuilders Limited, Larsen & Toubro (L&T) Shipbuilding, Bharati Shipyard, Hindustan Shipyard Limited, Garden Reach Shipbuilders & Engineers, Geometrica, Wilhelmsen Ships Service, Bureau Veritas, Shipping Companies (e.g., Maersk Line, MSC), Offshore Oil and Gas Companies (e.g., ONGC, Schlumberger), Naval Architecture Firms, Research Institutions (e.g., Indian Institute of Technology (IIT) in Marine Engineering). Defense Research and Development Organization (DRDO)

52. Market Research Analyst

A market research analyst studies market conditions to examine potential sales of a product or service, helping companies understand consumer preferences and trends. They gather and analyze data on competitors, market size, and customer demographics to inform strategic decisions and optimize marketing efforts.

"Market research analysts are the architects of insight, building strategies that connect products to the hearts and minds of consumers."

Where you can work: Nielsen, Kantar, Ipsos, Market Research Society (MRS), GfK. Deloitte, McKinsey & Company, PwC (PricewaterhouseCoopers), Accenture, TNS Global, ZebraTechnologies, Qualtrics, Mintel, Statista, Gartner, IDC, Forrester, Zinnov, KPMG, Deloitte

53. Materials Engineer

A materials engineer develops, tests, and evaluates materials used in a wide range of products, from metals and plastics to ceramics and composites. They focus on improving material performance, durability, and sustainability while ensuring that products meet industry standards and specifications.

"Materials engineers are the innovators of the future, transforming raw elements into advanced solutions that drive technology and industry forward."

Where you can work: Tata Steel, Bharat Forge, Larsen & Toubro (L&T), Reliance Industries Limited, Mahindra & Mahindra, ISRO (Indian Space Research Organization), DRDO (Defense Research and Development Organization), Hindalco Industries Limited, Saint-Gobain, Nirma Group, Steel Authority of India Limited (SAIL), Jindal Steel and Power, 3M India

54. Mechanical Engineer

A mechanical engineer designs, analyzes, and improves mechanical systems and devices, applying principles of physics and materials science to solve engineering challenges. They work across various industries, including automotive, aerospace, manufacturing, and energy, to create efficient and innovative solutions that enhance product performance and reliability.

"Mechanical engineers are the builders of innovation, transforming ideas into tangible solutions that power the world."

Where you can work: Tata Motors, Mahindra & Mahindra, Bharat Heavy Electricals Limited (BHEL), General Electric (GE), Siemens, Larsen & Toubro (L&T), Hindustan Aeronautics Limited (HAL), Bosch, Caterpillar Inc., Ford Motor Company, Ashok Leyland, Maruti Suzuki, Honeywell, Wipro (Engineering Services), Schneider

55. Mining Engineer

A mining engineer plans, develops, and operates mines while ensuring safe, efficient, and environmentally responsible mineral extraction. They assess mineral resources, design mine layouts, and implement extraction processes while adhering to safety regulations and sustainability practices.

"Mining engineers delve into the earth, unlocking its treasures while championing safety and sustainability in every excavation."

Where you can work: Coal India Limited, Vedanta Resources, Hindustan Zinc, Rio Tinto, BHP Billiton, National Mineral Development Corporation (NMDC), Essar Group, Adani Group, Sesa Goa, Jindal Steel and Power, De Beers Group, Newmont Mining Corporation, Barrick Gold, Southern Copper Corporation

56. Multimedia Programmer

A multimedia programmer designs and develops interactive multimedia applications, combining text, graphics, audio, and video to create engaging user experiences. They utilize programming languages and tools to bring concepts to life across platforms, including web, mobile, and games, enhancing communication and storytelling through technology.

"Multimedia programmers are the digital storytellers, weaving technology and creativity to craft immersive experiences that captivate audiences."

Where you can work: Adobe Systems, Unity Technologies, Electronic Arts (EA), NVIDIA, Ubisoft, Game Loft, Walt Disney Animation Studios, Pixar Animation Studios, BBC Interactive, Autodesk, Accenture Interactive, Cognizant, Infosys, Tata Consultancy Services (TCS), Wipro Digital

57. Naturopathic Doctor

A naturopathic doctor focuses on holistic approaches to health and wellness, using natural remedies and therapies to promote healing and prevent disease. They emphasize the body's inherent ability to heal itself, integrating treatments like herbal medicine, nutrition, and lifestyle counseling to support overall well-being.

"Naturopathic doctors are the guides to natural healing, nurturing the body's innate wisdom with the power of nature."

Where you can work: Private Naturopathic Clinics, Health Centers, Wellness Retreats, Natural Health Product Companies, Health Food Stores, Hospitals with Integrative Medicine Departments, Fitness Centers and Spas, Naturopathic Medical Schools, Naturopathic Associations, Pharmaceutical Companies, Insurance Companies (as consultants for alternative therapies)

58. Nurse

A nurse provides essential healthcare services, delivering compassionate patient care, administering treatments, and supporting individuals through their medical journeys. They play a crucial role in health education, patient advocacy, and the coordination of care across various healthcare settings.

"Nurses are the heart of healthcare, combining science and compassion to heal and support patients in their times of need."

Where you can work: Hospitals (e.g., Apollo Hospitals, Fortis Healthcare), Clinics (e.g., urgent care, family practice), Nursing Homes and Assisted Living Facilities, Home Healthcare Agencies, Public Health Departments, School Health Programs, Research Institutions, Military and Defense Services, Telehealth Services Pharmaceutical Companies (as clinical research nurses), Health Insurance Companies, Non-Profit Organizations (focused on health education and advocacy), Rehabilitation Centers, Dialysis Centers, Community Health Clinics

59. Optometrist

An optometrist is a healthcare professional who specializes in the examination, diagnosis, and treatment of visual disorders and eye diseases. They prescribe corrective lenses, provide vision therapy, and educate patients on eye health to enhance overall vision and well-being.

"Optometrists are the guardians of sight, blending science and care to help individuals see the world clearly."

Where you can work: Private Eye Care Clinics, Hospitals with Eye Care Departments, Optometric Associations, University Eye Clinics, Optical Retail Stores, Ophthalmology Practices, Community Health Centers, Military Healthcare Facilities, Insurance Companies (vision care departments), Research Institutions (In vision science)

60. Patent Attorney

A patent attorney specializes in intellectual property law, particularly in the protection and enforcement of patents. They provide legal guidance to inventors and businesses on patent application processes, litigation, and the strategic management of intellectual property rights.

"Patent attorneys are the architects of innovation, safeguarding ideas and inventions to foster creativity and progress."

Where you can work: Intellectual Property Law Firms, Corporate Legal Departments, Research and Development Organizations, Universities and Research Institutions, Government Patent Offices (e.g., United States Patent and Trademark Office), Technology Companies (e.g., Apple, Google, IBM), Biotechnology and Pharmaceutical Companies (e.g., Pfizer, Johnson & Johnson), Consulting Firms (specializing in intellectual property), Startups and Innovation Hubs, Trade Associations (focusing on patent law advocacy), Non-profit Organizations (in intellectual property awareness), Patent Brokerage Firms, In-house Counsel for Manufacturing Companies, Legal Aid Organizations (focused on intellectual property issues)

61. Petroleum Engineer

A petroleum engineer specializes in the exploration, extraction, and production of oil and natural gas resources. They design and implement methods to improve oil recovery and ensure the safe and efficient operation of drilling operations.

"Petroleum engineers are the pioneers of energy, harnessing natural resources to fuel progress and innovation."

Where you can work: ExxonMobil, Chevron, Royal Dutch Shell, BP (British Petroleum), Total Energies, ConocoPhillips, Halliburton, Schlumberger, Baker Hughes, Oxy Petroleum, ENI, Apache Corporation, Marathon Oil, Occidental Petroleum, Petrobras

62. Pharmaceutical Engineer

A pharmaceutical engineer focuses on the design and development of processes for the manufacture of pharmaceutical products, ensuring that medications are produced safely, efficiently, and in compliance with regulatory standards. They work on the formulation, production, and quality assurance of drugs, combining principles of engineering, chemistry, and biology to enhance healthcare outcomes.

"Pharmaceutical engineers bridge science and innovation, transforming ideas into life-saving medicines that improve global health."

Where you can work: Pfizer, Johnson & Johnson, Merck & Co., AbbVie, Roche, Bristol-Myers Squibb, GlaxoSmithKline (GSK), AstraZeneca, Novartis, Sanofi, Amgen, Eli Lilly and Company, Teva Pharmaceutical Industries, Baxter International, Gilead Sciences

63. Pharmacist

A pharmacist is a healthcare professional who specializes in the preparation, dispensation, and proper utilization of medications. They play a crucial role in patient care by providing drug information, counseling patients on medication use, and ensuring the safe and effective delivery of pharmaceutical care.

"Pharmacists are the medication experts, empowering patients with knowledge and ensuring their health through safe and effective drug therapy."

Where you can work: CVS Health, Walgreens Boots Alliance, Rite Aid, Walmart Pharmacy, Kroger Pharmacy, Target Pharmacy, Express Scripts, OptumRx, Mayo Clinic, Cleveland Clinic, Pharmaceutical Companies (e.g., Pfizer, Merck), Hospital Pharmacies, Community Health Centers, Long-term Care Facilities, Government Health Agencies

65. Physiotherapist

A physiotherapist specializes in restoring movement and function when someone is affected by injury, illness, or disability. They use personalized treatments and exercises to enhance recovery and improve quality of life.

"Empowering mobility, transforming lives."

Where you can work: Apollo Hospitals, Fortis Healthcare, Max Healthcare, Medanta, Narayana Health, Cloudnine Hospitals, AIIMS, Wockhardt Hospitals, CARE Hospitals, Columbia Asia Hospitals

65. Polymer / Plastic Engineer

A polymer/plastic engineer develops materials and products from polymers or plastics, emphasizing innovation and sustainability. They work on creating durable, lightweight, and eco-friendly solutions for various industries.

"Where science meets creativity in every molecule."

Where you can work: Reliance Industries, Indian Oil Corporation Limited (IOCL), BASF India, SABIC, Bayer India, ExxonMobil, SRF Limited, Haldia Petrochemicals, DuPont India, UFlex Ltd.

66. Product Designer

A product designer creates functional and visually appealing products by blending creativity with user-centered design principles. They focus on solving problems and enhancing user experiences through innovative and practical solutions.

"Designing products that inspire, solve, and delight."

Where you can work: Apple, Samsung Design, IDEO, Frog Design, Tata Elxsi, Philips Design, Google, Amazon

67. Production Engineer

A production engineer optimizes manufacturing processes to enhance efficiency, reduce costs, and ensure quality in production. They play a vital role in maintaining seamless operations and driving innovation in industrial systems.

"Engineering precision, powering productivity."

Where you can work: Tata Steel, Larsen & Toubro (L&T), Reliance Industries, Mahindra & Mahindra, Maruti Suzuki, Hindustan Unilever Limited (HUL), Bosch India, Bharat Heavy Electricals Limited (BHEL), Siemens India, Godrej & Boyce, Ashok Leyland, Hindalco Industries, JSW Steel, General Electric (GE), Aditya Birla Group

68. Psychologist

A psychologist studies human behavior and mental processes to understand, diagnose, and treat emotional or psychological challenges. They work to improve mental health, enhance well-being, and foster personal growth in individuals.

"Helping you become the best version of yourself."

Where you can work: Fortis Healthcare, Apollo Hospitals, Max Healthcare, Tata Institute of Social Sciences (TISS), AIIMS (All India Institute of Medical Sciences), Manipal Hospitals, Medanta, Wockhardt Hospitals, National Institute of Mental Health and Neurosciences (NIMHANS, CARE Hospitals, Hindustan Unilever Limited (HUL) – HR and Employee Well-being Departments, Accenture – Mental Health and Well-being Programs

69. Radiographer

A radiographer uses advanced imaging technology such as X-rays, CT scans, and MRIs to assist in diagnosing and treating medical conditions. They play a crucial role in healthcare by ensuring accurate imaging and patient safety.

"Imaging the unseen, diagnosing the unknown."

Where you can work: Apollo Hospitals, Fortis Healthcare, Max Healthcare, AIIMS (All India Institute of Medical Sciences), Medanta, Narayana Health, Wockhardt Hospitals, Tata Memorial Hospital, Manipal Hospitals, Columbia Asia Hospitals, CARE Hospitals, Sir Ganga Ram Hospital, HCG Hospitals, Rainbow Hospitals, Kokilaben Dhirubhai Ambani Hospital

70. Robotics Engineer

A robotic engineer designs, builds, and maintains robots to perform tasks that are difficult or dangerous for humans. They integrate mechanical, electrical, and software engineering principles to develop cutting-edge robotic systems for various industries.

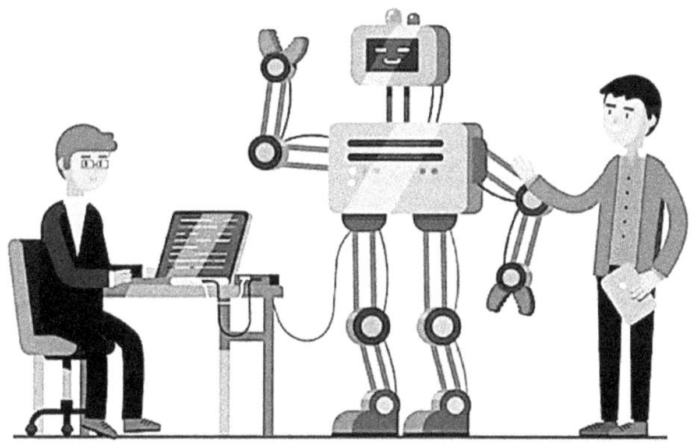

"Designing robots to think, learn, and evolve."

Where you can work: ABB, Boston Dynamics, FANUC Corporation, KUKA Robotics, iRobot, Tesla, Yaskawa Electric Corporation, Siemens, Hyundai Robotics, Universal Robots, Denso Robotics, Comau, Mitsubishi Electric, Rockwell Automation, Cyberdyne Inc.

71. Rubber Technologist

A rubber technologist specializes in the study and application of rubber materials, focusing on their production, processing, and quality control. They work to develop innovative solutions, improve rubber-based products, and ensure their durability and performance.

"Innovating with rubber, shaping the future of materials."

Where you can work: MRF Limited, Apollo Tyres, JK Tyre & Industries, Bridgestone India, Michelin India, Continental India, Goodyear India, Birla Carbon, Reliance Industries, Ceat Tyres, Exide Industries, Rubber Research Institute of India, Trelleborg Group, Continental ContiTech, Thermax

72. Safety Manager

A safety manager is responsible for developing and enforcing policies to ensure workplace safety, reducing risks, and complying with health and safety regulations. They identify hazards, implement safety programs, and promote a culture of safety across organizations.

"Safety is everyone's responsibility, and every life matters."

Where you can work: L&T (Larsen & Toubro), Tata Steel, Reliance Industries, NTPC Limited, BPCL (Bharat Petroleum Corporation Limited), ONGC (Oil and Natural Gas Corporation), Indian Oil Corporation Limited (IOCL), Shell India, Hindustan Zinc, Adani Group, Siemens India, Bosch India, UltraTech Cement, Godrej & Boyce

73. Sociologist

A sociologist studies human society, its structures, and relationships to understand social behavior and address societal issues. They analyze social problems, contribute to policy-making, and help improve community welfare through research and data analysis.

"Understanding society, shaping a better tomorrow."

Where you can work: Tata Institute of Social Sciences (TISS), UNDP (United Nations Development Programme), World Bank, National Institute of Urban Affairs (NIUA), Reliance Foundation, PwC (PricewaterhouseCoopers), KPMG, Accenture, Nielsen, Indian Council of Social Science Research (ICSSR), ActionAid India, Oxfam India, Centre for Social Research, Indian Government Ministries (e.g., Ministry of Social Justice and Empowerment), Social Impact Consulting Firms

74. Software Programmer

A software programmer writes, tests, and maintains code that allows computer applications to function. They are skilled in various programming languages and work on developing software solutions to meet user needs and solve complex problems.

"Code the future, create endless possibilities."

Where you can work: Microsoft, Google, Apple, Amazon, IBM, Oracle, Accenture, Infosys, TCS (Tata Consultancy Services), HCL, Wipro, Cognizant, Capgemini, SAP, Adobe, Facebook (Meta)

75. Sound Engineer

A sound engineer works with the technical aspects of sound, including recording, mixing, and editing audio for various media. They ensure high-quality audio production for music, film, television, and live events.

"Shaping sound, creating unforgettable experiences."

Where you can work: Sony Music Entertainment, Universal Music Group, Warner Music Group, Dolby Laboratories, BBC (British Broadcasting Corporation), Paramount Pictures, Lucasfilm, Pixar Animation Studios, Live Nation Entertainment, Red Bull Media House, EA Sports, Audio-Technica, Avid Technology, SoundOnSound, SpotifyFacebook (Meta)

76. Special Needs Teacher

A special needs teacher is dedicated to providing educational support and tailored learning experiences for students with physical, emotional, or cognitive disabilities. They create individualized programs that cater to the specific needs of each student, promoting growth and learning.

"Empathy in education, where every student matters."

Where you can work: The National Institute for the Empowerment of Persons with Disabilities (NIEPID), Sweekar Academy of Rehabilitation, Tata Institute of Social Sciences (TISS), The Association for the Welfare of Handicapped (AWH), Bhartiya Vidya Bhavan, M. S. Swaminathan Research Foundation, The Akshaya Patra Foundation, National Association of Special Education Teachers (NASET), Bangalore-based SPARC (Special Needs) School, Aditya Birla Integrated School, Keshav Memorial School, All Special needs Schools

77. Statistician

A statistician uses mathematical and statistical methods to collect, analyze, and interpret data, helping organizations make informed decisions. They work across various industries, applying statistical models to solve complex problems and predict future trends.

"Data tells the story, statistics reveal the truth."

Where you can work: IBM, Google, Amazon, Accenture, Nielsen, KPMG, Deloitte, Tata Consultancy Services (TCS), Wipro, PwC, Facebook (Meta), Microsoft, United Nations, European Union, Bank of America

78. Stock Broker

A stock broker is a professional who facilitates the buying and selling of financial securities, such as stocks and bonds, on behalf of clients. They offer investment advice, execute trades, and help clients navigate the complexities of the financial markets.

"Navigating the markets, unlocking investment potential."

Where you can work: Morgan Stanley, Goldman Sachs, JPMorgan Chase, HSBC, Citigroup, ICICI Securities, HDFC Securities, Kotak Securities, Axis Securities, SBI Securities, Edelweiss Financial Services, Angel One, Sharekhan, Zerodha. Upstox

79. Structural Engineer

A structural engineer designs and analyzes buildings, bridges, and other infrastructure to ensure they are safe, stable, and capable of withstanding external forces. They work on creating resilient structures while considering safety, sustainability, and functionality.

"Engineering solutions that transform ideas into landmarks."

Where you can work: L&T (Larsen & Toubro), Tata Projects, Jacobs Engineering, AECOM, Buro Happold, Arup Group, WSP Global, Ramboll, Atkins Global, Fluor Corporation, KPMG, GHD Group, Turner Construction, Systra, Mott MacDonald

80. Surveyor

A surveyor is a professional who measures and maps land, air, and water bodies, helping to define property boundaries, land features, and construction sites. They use specialized tools and technology to ensure accurate data collection for planning, development, and legal purposes.

"Surveying the land, shaping tomorrow's skyline."

Where you can work: AECOM, Jacobs Engineering, WSP Global, GHD Group, Arup Group, CBRE Group, L&T Construction, Turner & Townsend, Buro Happold, Knight Frank, RICS (Royal Institution of Chartered Surveyors), TATA Projects, Atkins Global, Colliers International, Jones Lang Lasalle (JLL)

81. Teacher

A teacher is a professional who imparts knowledge, fosters intellectual and emotional growth, and helps students develop essential life skills. They create an engaging learning environment that encourages curiosity, critical thinking, and creativity.

"Teaching is the most powerful tool to change the world."

Where you can work: Government / Private / International Schools & Colleges, Pearson Education, Educomp Solutions, Byju's, NIIT, Tata ClassEdge, The British Council, Educational Institutes, Coaching Centers

82. Technical Writer

A technical writer creates clear, concise, and accurate documentation that explains complex technical information to a non-technical audience. They produce manuals, user guides, and online help resources to assist users in understanding and using products or services effectively.

"Turning complexity into clarity through words."

Where you can work: IBM, Microsoft, Google, Amazon, Oracle, Adobe, Cisco Systems, Atlassian, Dell Technologies, Red Hat, SAP, Hewlett-Packard (HP), Accenture, Salesforce, TechSmith

83. Telecommunication Engineer

A telecommunications engineer designs, installs, and maintains communication systems, including telephones, internet, and satellite networks. They ensure that telecommunication infrastructure operates smoothly and efficiently, meeting the needs of both businesses and consumers.

"Telecommunications: the backbone of global connectivity."

Where you can work: Ericsson, Nokia, Huawei Technologies, Cisco Systems, Qualcomm, ZTE Corporation, AT&T, Vodafone, T-Mobile, Reliance Jio, Bharti Airtel, Vodafone Idea, Comcast, Huawei, Juniper Networks

84. Thermal Engineer

A Thermal Engineer specializes in the design, analysis, and optimization of systems that involve heat transfer and energy conversion, ensuring efficiency and sustainability across various industries.

"Mastering the Science of Heat and Energy"

Where you can work: General Electric (GE), Siemens, Honeywell, Bosch, Cummins, Mitsubishi Heavy Industries, Rolls-Royce, United Technologies, ABB, Ford Motor Company

85. Translator

A translator converts written content from one language to another, ensuring the original meaning, tone, and context are preserved. They work with a variety of content, including documents, websites, books, and technical materials, bridging language barriers for communication and understanding.

"Turning words into understanding, across languages."

Where you can work: Lionbridge, TransPerfect, SDL, Moravia, RWS, Welocalize, Vistatec, Appen, Keywords Studios, Gengo, Toppan Digital Language, One Hour Translation, Morningside Translations, GlobalLink Translation, Straker Translations

86. Transportation Engineer

A transportation engineer plans and manages systems for moving people and goods efficiently, safely, and sustainably. They work on transportation infrastructure such as roads, bridges, railways, and airports to ensure smooth and effective movement of traffic.

"Bridging distances, connecting people."

Where you can work: AECOM, Jacobs Engineering, WSP Global, Arup Group, Bechtel Corporation, Parsons Corporation, Fluor Corporation, Hatch Ltd., HDR Inc., KBR Inc., Atkins Global, Tetra Tech, Turner Construction, Ramboll Group, Mott MacDonald, Morningside Translations, GlobalLink Translation, Straker Translations

87. UX Designer

A UX (User Experience) Designer focuses on enhancing the usability and overall experience of digital products, ensuring that users can easily interact with them. They research, design, and test user interfaces to create seamless, engaging, and intuitive experiences.

"Designing experiences that connect people to products."

Where you can work: Google, Apple, Microsoft, Amazon, Facebook, Adobe, IBM, Uber, Airbnb, Tesla, Netflix, Slack Technologies, Pinterest, LinkedIn, Salesforce

88. Veterinary Doctor

A veterinary doctor diagnoses and treats animals, ranging from household pets to livestock, ensuring their health and well-being. They provide medical care, perform surgeries, and advise pet owners and animal organizations on the best care practices.

"Caring for animals, protecting lives."

Where you can work: Indian Veterinary Research Institute (IVRI), National Dairy Development Board (NDDB), Amul, Nestlé Purina PetCare, Hindustan Unilever, Pet Hospital, Animal Care Hospitals, Petcare centers

89. Video Editor

A video editor is responsible for assembling raw footage, audio, and special effects into a final product that communicates a message or story. They work with filmmakers, content creators, and brands to craft visually appealing and engaging videos.

"Turning raw footage into compelling stories, one frame at a time."

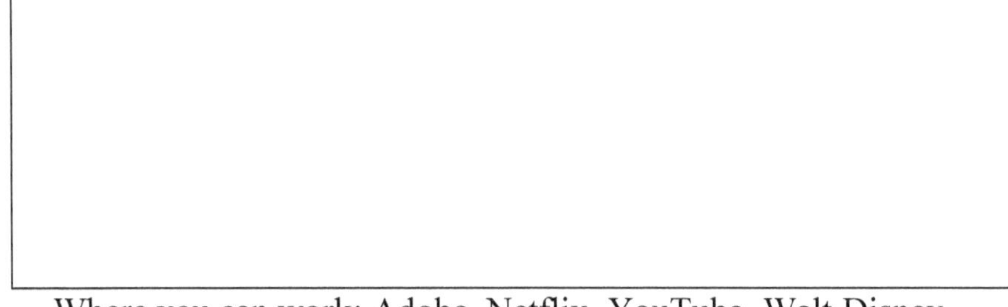

Where you can work: Adobe, Netflix, YouTube, Walt Disney Studios, NBCUniversal, ViacomCBS, Warner Bros., Sony Pictures Entertainment, BBC Studios, Discovery Channel, Pixar Animation Studios, DreamWorks Animation, Hulu, Lionsgate, Paramount Pictures

90. VLSI Chip Designer

A VLSI (Very Large-Scale Integration) / Chip Designer specializes in designing integrated circuits, including microchips and processors, used in various electronic devices. They use specialized software and tools to create efficient, high-performance circuits that are integral to modern technology.

"Designing the chips that power the future."

Where you can work: Intel, Qualcomm, AMD, NVIDIA, Texas Instruments, Broadcom, Samsung Semiconductor, TSMC (Taiwan Semiconductor Manufacturing Company), Micron Technology, ARM Holdings, Analog Devices, STMicroelectronics, Xilinx, MediaTek, Marvell Technology

Chapter 4: Emerging New Careers In AI

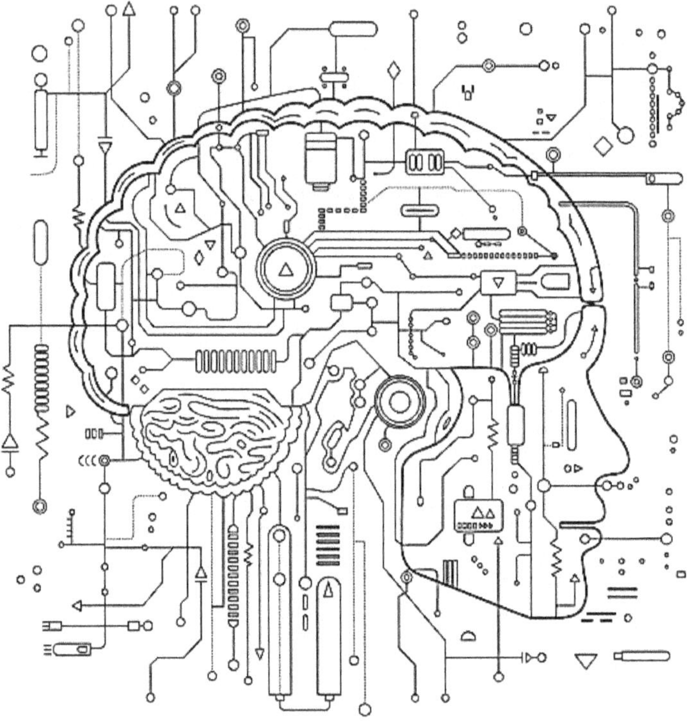

Artificial Intelligence (AI) offers a diverse range of career opportunities across industries. Here are some prominent job roles in AI, categorized by their focus and responsibilities

1. Core AI Development Roles

a. Machine Learning Engineer

- **Responsibilities**: Build and deploy machine learning models, optimize algorithms, and develop predictive systems.
- **Skills Required**: Python, R, TensorFlow, PyTorch, Scikit-learn, mathematics, and statistics.

b. Data Scientist

- **Responsibilities**: Analyze and interpret complex data, build predictive models, and generate actionable insights.
- **Skills Required**: Data analysis, SQL, Python, R, machine learning, and visualization tools like Tableau or Power BI.

c. AI Research Scientist

- **Responsibilities**: Conduct research to advance AI technologies, publish papers, and innovate algorithms and models.
- **Skills Required**: Deep learning, reinforcement learning, natural language processing, and mathematical modeling.

d. AI/ML Developer

- **Responsibilities**: Design and implement AI-powered applications, often integrated with existing software solutions.
- **Skills Required**: Programming, software development, APIs, and AI frameworks.

2. Data-Oriented Roles

a. Data Engineer

- **Responsibilities**: Design and maintain data pipelines and infrastructure for AI models.
- **Skills Required**: ETL processes, Hadoop, Spark, NoSQL, and SQL databases.

b. Big Data Engineer

- **Responsibilities**: Handle large datasets, manage data storage solutions, and ensure scalability for AI systems.
- **Skills Required**: Apache Hadoop, Spark, Hive, and cloud platforms like AWS or Azure.

---

3. Specialized AI Roles

a. Natural Language Processing (NLP) Engineer

- **Responsibilities**: Develop systems for text and speech recognition, language translation, and chatbots.
- **Skills Required**: NLP libraries like SpaCy, NLTK, transformers, and linguistic analysis.

b. Computer Vision Engineer

- **Responsibilities**: Create systems for image recognition, object detection, facial recognition, and video analysis.
- **Skills Required**: OpenCV, CNNs, PyTorch, TensorFlow, and image processing.

c. Robotics Engineer

- **Responsibilities**: Develop AI algorithms for autonomous robots, drones, and industrial automation.

- **Skills Required**: ROS, Python, C++, sensors, and robotics hardware.

d. Deep Learning Engineer

- **Responsibilities**: Build deep learning models using neural networks for applications like speech recognition and medical imaging.
- **Skills Required**: TensorFlow, Keras, PyTorch, and GPU optimization.

---

4. Applied AI Roles

a. AI Product Manager

- **Responsibilities**: Oversee AI projects, define product requirements, and manage cross-functional teams.
- **Skills Required**: Project management, business acumen, and AI understanding.

b. AI Ethicist

- **Responsibilities**: Ensure ethical development and deployment of AI systems, focusing on fairness, bias, and privacy.
- **Skills Required**: Ethics, policy understanding, and data analysis.

c. Business Intelligence Developer

- **Responsibilities**: Implement AI to enhance decision-making and business operations.
- **Skills Required**: Data visualization, predictive modeling, and analytics.

---

5. Supportive and Hybrid Roles

a. AI Consultant

- **Responsibilities**: Provide AI solutions to businesses, including strategy, implementation, and optimization.
- **Skills Required**: AI knowledge, communication, and problem-solving.

b. AI Trainer

- **Responsibilities**: Train AI systems using labelled data to improve their performance.
- **Skills Required**: Data annotation, domain knowledge, and accuracy verification.

c. Cloud AI Engineer

- **Responsibilities**: Deploy AI solutions on cloud platforms like AWS, Azure, or Google Cloud.
- **Skills Required**: Cloud services, DevOps, and AI integration.

d. AI Educator/Trainer

- **Responsibilities**: Teach AI concepts and skills to aspiring professionals.
- **Skills Required**: Knowledge of AI, public speaking, and curriculum development.

6. AI in Business and Management

a. AI Strategist

- **Responsibilities**: Develop AI-driven strategies to enhance business operations and decision-making.
- **Skills Required**: Business analytics, AI application frameworks, and strategic planning.

b. Chief AI Officer (CAIO)

- **Responsibilities**: Oversee AI adoption and innovation across an organization.
- **Skills Required**: Leadership, technical expertise, and AI vision.

c. AI Policy Specialist

- **Responsibilities**: Develop guidelines and policies to regulate AI use within organizations or governments.
- **Skills Required**: Knowledge of AI ethics, regulations, and governance.

---

7. AI in Creative and Media Industries

a. Creative AI Engineer

- **Responsibilities**: Develop AI tools for content creation, such as image generation, music composition, and video editing.
- **Skills Required**: Generative models (GANs), NLP, and creative design tools.

b. AI Game Developer

- **Responsibilities**: Use AI to create intelligent NPCs, adaptive gameplay, and realistic environments in video games.
- **Skills Required**: Game engines (Unity, Unreal), reinforcement learning, and Python/C++.

c. Virtual Reality (VR) and Augmented Reality (AR) Specialist

- **Responsibilities**: Combine AI with VR/AR for immersive applications in gaming, training, and simulation.
- **Skills Required**: AI, 3D modeling, and AR/VR frameworks.

---

8. AI in Healthcare

a. Medical Imaging Specialist

- **Responsibilities**: Develop AI systems for diagnostics through imaging technologies like CT, MRI, and X-rays.
- **Skills Required**: Deep learning, medical datasets, and computer vision.

b. Bioinformatics Scientist

- **Responsibilities**: Use AI to analyze biological data for genomics, drug discovery, and personalized medicine.
- **Skills Required**: Bioinformatics tools, AI algorithms, and data science.

c. Healthcare AI Consultant

- **Responsibilities**: Implement AI solutions in healthcare settings to optimize patient care and operations.
- **Skills Required**: Domain knowledge, AI tools, and consulting expertise.

---

9. AI in Security and Defense

a. Cybersecurity Specialist (AI-focused)

- **Responsibilities**: Develop AI systems to detect and prevent cyberattacks, including intrusion detection and malware analysis.
- **Skills Required**: AI algorithms, security protocols, and ethical hacking.

b. Defense AI Engineer

- **Responsibilities**: Create AI-based defense systems for surveillance, reconnaissance, and automated drones.
- **Skills Required**: Robotics, AI, and military applications.

10. AI in Education

a. EdTech AI Developer

- **Responsibilities**: Build AI-driven learning platforms, personalized education tools, and virtual tutors.
- **Skills Required**: NLP, personalization algorithms, and pedagogy.

b. Curriculum Designer (AI-focused)

- **Responsibilities**: Develop courses on AI for schools, colleges, and professional training.
- **Skills Required**: AI knowledge, teaching, and instructional design.

11. AI in Sustainability and Environment

a. Environmental AI Analyst

- **Responsibilities**: Use AI to model climate change, predict natural disasters, and optimize resource usage.
- **Skills Required**: AI algorithms, GIS, and environmental science.

b. Smart City AI Specialist

- **Responsibilities**: Develop AI-driven solutions for urban planning, traffic management, and energy efficiency.
- **Skills Required**: IoT, AI, and urban studies.

12. AI in Finance

a. Financial Analyst (AI-powered)

- **Responsibilities**: Leverage AI for stock market prediction, fraud detection, and risk assessment.
- **Skills Required**: Machine learning, quantitative analysis, and financial modeling.

b. Algorithmic Trading Engineer

- **Responsibilities**: Develop AI algorithms for automated stock trading and investment management.
- **Skills Required**: Financial data analysis, programming, and deep learning.

c. Fraud Detection Specialist

- **Responsibilities**: Create systems to identify fraudulent activities in banking and insurance.
- **Skills Required**: Pattern recognition, anomaly detection, and domain expertise.

13. AI in Manufacturing

a. Industrial Automation Specialist

- **Responsibilities**: Use AI for predictive maintenance, quality control, and robotic process automation (RPA).
- **Skills Required**: AI, robotics, and mechanical systems.

b. Supply Chain Analyst (AI-focused)

- **Responsibilities**: Optimize logistics and supply chain operations using AI and predictive analytics.
- **Skills Required**: AI models, logistics, and optimization.

14. AI in Energy

a. Smart Grid Specialist

- **Responsibilities**: Develop AI solutions for efficient energy distribution and consumption.
- **Skills Required**: AI algorithms, electrical engineering, and renewable energy.

b. Renewable Energy Analyst

- **Responsibilities**: Use AI to improve efficiency in solar, wind, and other renewable energy systems.
- **Skills Required**: AI, simulation tools, and environmental science.

15. AI in Transportation

a. Autonomous Vehicle Engineer

- **Responsibilities**: Develop AI systems for self-driving cars, drones, and other autonomous vehicles.
- **Skills Required**: AI, sensors, and control systems.

b. Traffic Management Specialist

- **Responsibilities**: Use AI to optimize traffic flow and reduce congestion.
- **Skills Required**: Data analysis, AI, and urban planning.

16. AI in Marketing and Customer Experience

a. AI Marketing Specialist

- **Responsibilities**: Use AI to personalize customer experiences, optimize marketing campaigns, and analyze consumer behavior.
- **Skills Required**: AI algorithms, marketing analytics, and data visualization tools.

b. Customer Support AI Engineer

- **Responsibilities**: Build AI-based chatbots and virtual assistants to provide efficient customer support.
- **Skills Required**: Natural Language Processing (NLP), deep learning, and conversational AI.

c. Marketing Analytics Manager

- **Responsibilities**: Analyze large-scale marketing data with AI tools to optimize strategies and track KPIs.
- **Skills Required**: Data science, machine learning, and marketing automation.

---

17. AI in Legal and Compliance

a. Legal AI Specialist

- **Responsibilities**: Develop AI-driven solutions to automate contract review, document analysis, and legal research.
- **Skills Required**: NLP, legal domain expertise, and machine learning.

b. AI Compliance Officer

- **Responsibilities**: Ensure AI systems and implementations follow regulatory standards and ethical guidelines.

- **Skills Required**: Knowledge of AI regulations, ethics, and compliance frameworks.

---

18. AI in Telecommunications

a. Telecommunications AI Engineer

- **Responsibilities**: Apply AI to optimize network performance, traffic management, and predictive maintenance in telecom systems.
- **Skills Required**: AI, networking protocols, and telecom systems.

b. Network Automation Specialist

- **Responsibilities**: Develop AI systems to automate network monitoring, fault detection, and resource allocation in telecommunications.
- **Skills Required**: AI, network protocols, and automation tools.

---

19. AI in Manufacturing and Industry 4.0

a. AI-driven Quality Assurance Engineer

- **Responsibilities**: Develop AI models for defect detection, product quality analysis, and process optimization in manufacturing.
- **Skills Required**: Machine vision, deep learning, and industrial engineering.

b. Predictive Maintenance Engineer

- **Responsibilities**: Use AI to predict machinery breakdowns, reducing downtime and improving production efficiency.

- **Skills Required**: Time series analysis, sensor data processing, and machine learning.

20. AI in Agriculture

a. Precision Agriculture Scientist

- **Responsibilities**: Develop AI-based solutions for crop monitoring, yield prediction, and sustainable farming practices.
- **Skills Required**: AI, agriculture science, and geospatial data.

b. Agricultural Robotics Engineer

- **Responsibilities**: Design and develop robots powered by AI for tasks like planting, harvesting, and field monitoring.
- **Skills Required**: Robotics, AI, sensors, and automation.

21. AI in Space Exploration

a. Space Robotics Engineer

- **Responsibilities**: Develop AI-driven robots for space exploration, such as rover autonomy and satellite servicing.
- **Skills Required**: Robotics, AI, space science, and systems engineering.

b. Astronomical Data Scientist

- **Responsibilities**: Use AI to analyze vast amounts of data from telescopes, satellites, and space probes.
- **Skills Required**: Data science, AI algorithms, and astrophysics.

22. AI in Human Resources

a. AI Talent Acquisition Specialist

- **Responsibilities**: Use AI to enhance recruitment processes by automating candidate screening, sourcing, and matching.
- **Skills Required**: NLP, recruitment platforms, and HR technologies.

b. AI-driven Employee Experience Manager

- **Responsibilities**: Use AI to personalize employee development, engagement, and wellbeing programs.
- **Skills Required**: AI, HR analytics, and people management.

---

23. AI in Finance and Banking

a. AI Fraud Prevention Specialist

- **Responsibilities**: Develop AI systems to detect fraudulent transactions, identity theft, and financial crimes.
- **Skills Required**: Machine learning, anomaly detection, and financial analytics.

b. AI Risk Analyst

- **Responsibilities**: Use AI to assess financial risks, such as credit risk, market volatility, and portfolio management.
- **Skills Required**: Quantitative analysis, financial modeling, and AI tools.

c. Robo-Advisor Developer

- **Responsibilities**: Develop AI-based systems for automated investment advice and wealth management.
- **Skills Required**: Finance, algorithms, and machine learning.

24. AI in Social Media and Content Creation

a. Social Media AI Analyst

- **Responsibilities**: Apply AI to analyze social media data for insights into consumer behavior, trends, and sentiment.
- **Skills Required**: Data science, NLP, and sentiment analysis.

b. AI Content Generation Specialist

- **Responsibilities**: Use AI to generate written content, articles, blogs, or even video scripts.
- **Skills Required**: NLP, deep learning, and content strategy.

c. Influencer Marketing AI Analyst

- **Responsibilities**: Use AI to analyze influencer effectiveness, optimize partnerships, and predict campaign success.
- **Skills Required**: AI, social media analytics, and marketing strategies.

25. AI in Customer Analytics

a. AI-driven Customer Insights Analyst

- **Responsibilities**: Analyze customer behavior patterns, predict preferences, and help shape business strategies.
- **Skills Required**: AI, data analytics, and business intelligence.

b. Predictive Modeling Expert

- **Responsibilities**: Use AI to create models that predict future consumer behavior, trends, and purchasing patterns.
- **Skills Required**: Machine learning, time series analysis, and statistics.

26. AI in Environmental and Climate Science

a. Climate Modeling Scientist

- **Responsibilities**: Develop AI models to simulate and predict climate change and its impacts.
- **Skills Required**: AI, climate science, and geospatial data.

b. AI for Carbon Footprint Analysis

- **Responsibilities**: Apply AI to calculate and optimize carbon footprints across industries and organizations.
- **Skills Required**: AI, environmental science, and sustainability analytics.

27. AI in Retail and E-commerce

a. AI Supply Chain Optimization Specialist

- **Responsibilities**: Use AI to enhance inventory management, demand forecasting, and logistics operations in retail.
- **Skills Required**: AI, logistics, and business operations.

b. E-commerce Personalization Engineer

- **Responsibilities**: Build AI systems to recommend products, optimize search results, and personalize shopping experiences.
- **Skills Required**: Machine learning, data analytics, and e-commerce platforms.

28. AI in Arts and Entertainment

a. AI Music Composer

- **Responsibilities**: Use AI algorithms to compose music, generate soundtracks, and produce melodies.
- **Skills Required**: AI, music theory, and generative models (e.g., GANs).

b. AI-based Animation Artist

- **Responsibilities**: Apply AI techniques in creating lifelike animations and character behavior for films and video games.
- **Skills Required**: Animation, AI, and graphics tools.

---

29. AI in Consumer Electronics

a. AI-enabled Smart Device Developer

- **Responsibilities**: Create AI-based applications for smart devices like smartphones, wearables, and IoT devices.
- **Skills Required**: Embedded systems, AI, and device development.

b. Voice Interface Developer

- **Responsibilities**: Develop AI systems for voice-based interactions, such as virtual assistants (e.g., Siri, Alexa).
- **Skills Required**: NLP, speech recognition, and AI frameworks.

---

30. AI in Transportation and Logistics

a. Autonomous Drone Engineer

- **Responsibilities**: Develop AI-driven drones for delivery, monitoring, and surveillance applications.
- **Skills Required**: Robotics, machine learning, and drone technologies.

b. AI Fleet Manager

- **Responsibilities**: Use AI to optimize fleet management for delivery, ride-sharing, and logistics companies.
- **Skills Required**: AI, fleet management, and predictive analytics.

Other Emerging AI Roles

1. **AI Operations Specialist**: Manage the deployment and monitoring of AI systems in production.
2. **Generative AI Specialist**: Focus on building models like GPT for creative tasks such as content generation.
3. **AI Policy Analyst**: Develop policies for the ethical and legal use of AI technologies.
4. **AI Ethics and Bias Specialist:** Focus on mitigating bias and ensuring fairness in AI systems.
5. **Quantum Machine Learning Scientist:** Combine AI with quantum computing for next-gen solutions.
6. **AI Anthropologist:** Study the societal impact of AI on culture and human behavior.
7. **Generative AI Specialist:** Design creative AI applications in areas like art, music, and literature.
8. **AI Policy Analyst:** Understand and shape AI legislation and policies.
9. **AI Neuroscientist:** Research how AI can mimic the human brain and cognitive processes.

10. **AI Legal Advisor:** Provide legal advice on the implementation and ethics of AI systems.
11. **AI-augmented Artist:** Collaborate with AI to produce art, literature, and music.
12. **AI Hardware Engineer:** Design and optimize hardware specifically for AI workloads, such as GPUs, TPUs, and neuromorphic chips.
13. **AI Systems Architect:** Design the end-to-end architecture of scalable AI systems, integrating software, hardware, and networking.
14. **Explainable AI (XAI) Specialist:** Develop tools and methodologies to make AI systems transparent and interpretable.
15. **AI Curriculum Developer:** Design educational programs to train the next generation of AI professionals.
16. **Synthetic Data Scientist:** Create and manage synthetic datasets to train AI systems without relying on real-world data.
17. **AI Healthcare Strategist:** Develop AI-driven solutions to enhance diagnostics, patient care, and drug discovery.
18. **AI Agriculture Analyst**: Use AI for precision farming, crop monitoring, and supply chain optimization.
19. **AI Climate Scientist:** Leverage AI to model climate changes, predict disasters, and propose sustainability solutions.
20. **Autonomous Vehicle AI Specialist**: Develop AI systems for self-driving cars, drones, and other autonomous vehicles.
21. **AI Energy Analyst:** Design AI solutions for optimizing energy use and integrating renewable sources.
22. **Human-AI Collaboration Specialist:** Create systems that enable seamless collaboration between humans and AI.
23. **Conversational AI Designer:** Specialize in designing natural and engaging chatbot and voice assistant interactions.
24. **AI Behavioral Specialist:** Study and improve how AI interacts with humans, focusing on user experience and behavior modeling.
25. **AI-driven Gamification Designer:** Incorporate AI to design interactive, adaptive, and immersive game experiences.
26. **AI Governance Consultant:** Help organizations navigate the governance, compliance, and regulation of AI systems.
27. **AI Diversity and Inclusion Officer:** Ensure AI systems are inclusive and representative across diverse populations.
28. **AI Auditor:** Evaluate AI systems for compliance with ethical, legal, and operational standards.

29. **AI Disaster Response Analyst:** Develop AI solutions to aid in disaster prediction, preparation, and response.
30. **Edge AI Engineer:** Build AI models that run efficiently on edge devices, such as smartphones and IoT devices.
31. **Metaverse AI Specialist:** Develop AI technologies for virtual reality (VR) and augmented reality (AR) applications in the metaverse.
32. **AI Blockchain Engineer:** Integrate AI with blockchain technology for secure, decentralized applications.
33. **AI Cybersecurity Analyst:** Use AI to predict and prevent cybersecurity threats.
34. **AI Nanotechnology Specialist:** Combine AI with nanotechnology for advanced material and medical research.
35. **AI Business Strategist:** Develop AI-driven business models and strategies for competitive advantage.
36. **AI Risk Manager:** Assess and mitigate risks associated with AI deployment in business processes.
37. **AI Marketing Analyst:** Use AI to analyze consumer behavior, optimize marketing strategies, and predict trends.
38. **AI Financial Advisor:** Implement AI systems to optimize investment strategies and risk assessments.
39. **AI Knowledge Engineer:** Curate and organize domain-specific knowledge for AI reasoning systems.
40. **AI Robotics Engineer:** Design intelligent robots with advanced perception, decision-making, and interaction capabilities.
41. **AI Multimodal Specialist:** Focus on integrating text, image, audio, and video data for AI applications.
42. **AI Workflow Optimizer:** Optimize business processes using AI-based automation and analytics.
43. **AI Content Authenticity Specialist:** Develop systems to detect and prevent deepfakes or other AI-generated misuses.
44. **AI Integration Specialist**: Focuses on seamlessly incorporating AI solutions into existing business processes and systems to enhance efficiency and productivity.
45. **AI Product Manager:** Oversees the development and deployment of AI-driven products, ensuring they meet market needs and align with business objectives.
46. **AI Solutions Architect:** Designs comprehensive AI solutions tailored to specific business challenges, integrating various technologies and platforms.

47. **AI Trainer/Curator:** Develops and curates training data for AI models, ensuring quality and relevance to improve system performance.
48. **AI Chatbot Developer:** Specializes in creating intelligent conversational agents that enhance customer service and user engagement.
49. **AI Research Scientist:** Conducts advanced research to develop new AI algorithms and models, pushing the boundaries of what AI can achieve.
50. **AI Environmental Scientist:** Employs AI to model environmental changes, manage natural resources, and develop sustainable solutions.

Steps to Start a Career in AI

1. **Educational Path**: Obtain degrees in computer science, data science, or AI-related fields. Consider higher studies in AI or ML.
2. **Build a Portfolio**: Participate in AI challenges (e.g., Kaggle), AI related Hackathons, contribute to open-source projects, or complete AI-related coursework.
3. **Certifications & Courses**: Gain expertise with certifications in AI, deep learning, and specific tools
4. **Networking**: Attend AI conferences, webinars, and events to learn from experts and connect with industry leaders.

Chapter 5: Prompts for Discovering You

A **prompt** is a set of instructions, a question, or a statement given to Open AI's Chat GPT / Google Gemini / Microsoft Copilot / DeepSeek to guide them toward providing a specific response or performing a task.

❑ Open AI's Chat GPT https://chatgpt.com/

❑ Google Gemini https://gemini.google.com/

❑ Microsoft Copilot https://copilot.microsoft.com/

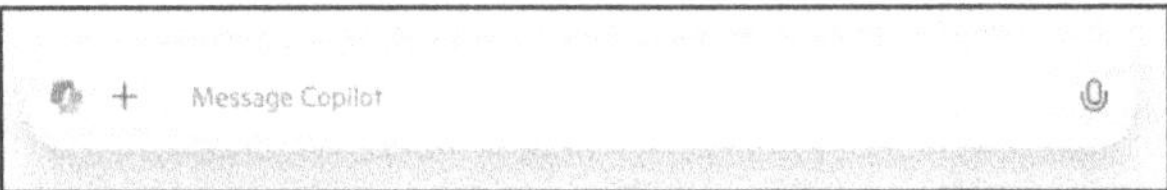

❑ DeepSeek https://www.deepseek.com/

Use 5W and 1H questions (Who, What, When, Where, Why, and How) to gather more details about the career.

Sample Prompts:

1. Who

- Who can pursue a career in aeronautical engineering?
- Who are the top employers in the aeronautical engineering field?
- Who are some notable aeronautical engineers in history?
- Who can guide me in choosing the right aeronautical engineering program?

2. What

- What does an aeronautical engineer do?
- What skills are essential to succeed as an aeronautical engineer?
- What are the differences between aeronautical and aerospace engineering?
- What industries hire aeronautical engineers?
- What certifications or degrees are required for aeronautical engineering?

3. When

- When should I start preparing for a career in aeronautical engineering?
- When can I expect to start earning as an aeronautical engineer?
- When is the best time to apply for internships in this field?
- When did aeronautical engineering gain prominence as a career field?

4. Where

- Where can I study aeronautical engineering?
- Where do aeronautical engineers typically work? (e.g., labs, manufacturing plants, space agencies)
- Where are the major aeronautical engineering hubs globally?
- Where can I find scholarships for aeronautical engineering programs?

5. Why

- Why should I choose aeronautical engineering as a career?
- Why is aeronautical engineering important for modern transportation and space exploration?
- Why is physics and mathematics critical for aeronautical engineering?
- Why are internships and hands-on projects important in this field?

6. How

- How do I become an aeronautical engineer?
- How much can I earn as an aeronautical engineer?
- How do I choose the right specialization within aeronautical engineering?
- How do aeronautical engineers contribute to the aviation industry?
- How can I stay updated on advancements in aeronautical technology?

Chapter 6: Career Journey

Tracks to Select after Discovery!

Track: Engineering/Technology/Architecture/Design

Degree	Profession
❑ B.Tech.(Bachelor of Technology) ❑ B.E. (Bachelor of Engineering) ❑ BF.Tech.(Bachelor of Fashion Technology) ❑ B.Arch. (Bachelor of Architecture) ❑ B.Plan (Bachelor of Planning) ❑ B.I.D (Bachelor of Interior Design) ❑ B.Des (Bachelor of Design)	Engineer, Mathematician, Scientist, Architect, Commercial Pilot, Astronaut, Naval Officer, Physicist, Statistician, Interior Designer, Fashion Designer, Automobile Designer, Town Planner, Chemist, Data Scientist, Artificial Intelligent Expert , Agriculturalist, Manufacturing expert etc.,

Branches in Engineering / Technology:

1. Aerospace

2. Agricultural & Food

3. Architecture

4. Automobile

5. Biochemical

6. Biological Sciences

7. Biotechnology

8. Ceramic

9. Chemical

10. Civil

11. Computer Science

12. Computer Science with Artificial Intelligence & Machine Learning

13. Computer Science with Data Science

14. Computer Science with Gamification

15. Computer Science with IoT

16. Computer Science with Business Systems

17. Computer Science with Cyber Security

18. Electrical Electronics

19. Electronics & Communication

20. Electronics & Electrical

21. Electronics & Electrical Communication

20. Electronics & Instrumentation

21. Engineering Physics

22. Engineering Science

23. Environmental Science

24. Industrial Instrumentation

25. Manufacturing Science

26. Marine

27. Materials Science

28. Mathematics & Computing

29. Mechanical

30. Medical Engineering

31. Metallurgical

32. Mineral

33. Mining

34. Mining Machinery

35. Naval Architecture

36. Ocean Engineering

37. Petroleum

38. Plastic

39. Polymer Science

40. Production

41. Textile Technology

Track: Medicine & Surgery / AYUSH - Ayurveda / Unani/ Siddha / Homeopathy, Agriculture, Allied Sciences, Paramedical/ Nursing/ Rehabilitation Science

Degree	Profession
❑ MBBS (Bachelor of Medicine & Bachelor of Surgery) ❑ BDS (Bachelor of Dental Surgery) ❑ BAMS (Bachelor of Ayurvedic Medicine & Surgery) ❑ BSMS (Bachelor of Siddha Medicine & Surgery) ❑ BNYS (Bachelor of Naturopathy & Yogic Sciences) ❑ BHMS (Bachelor of Homeopathic Medicine & Surgery) ❑ BUMS (Bachelor of Unani Medicine & Surgery)	Doctor: Anaesthetist Cardiologist Dermatologist Endocrinologist Gastroenterologist General Surgeon Gynaecologist Haematologist Neonatologist Nephrologist Neurologist Oncologist Ophthalmologist Orthopaedic Surgeon Otolaryngologist Paediatrician Pathologist Physician Psychiatrist Pulmonologist Radiologist Urologist Dentist Homeopathic Doctor Ayurvedic Doctor Naturopathic Doctor Unani Doctor

❑ B.Sc. (Nursing) (Bachelor of Science (Nursing))	Veterinary Doctor Nurse Optometrist Occupational Therapist Physiotherapist Trauma Therapist Pharmacist Orthotist/Prosthetist Audiology & Speech Therapist Rehabilitation Therapist Nutritionist and Dietician Microbiologist Agriculturist Seri culturist Aqua culturist Etc.
❑ B.Optom.(Bachelor of Optometry)	
❑ BOT (Bachelor of Occupational Therapy)	
❑ BPT (Bachelor of Physiotherapy)	
❑ B.Sc. (Trauma Care Management)	
❑ Pharm.D.(Doctor of Pharmacy)	
❑ B.Pharma (Bachelor of Pharmacy)	
❑ B.Pharm (Ayu)(Bachelor of Pharmacy(Ayurveda))	
❑ B.P.O (Bachelor in Prosthetics & Orthotics)	
❑ B.ASLP (Bachelor in Audiology & Speech Language pathology)	

❑ B.R.Sc.(Bachelor in Rehabilitation Science) ❑ B.Sc. (Agriculture) ❑ B.Sc.(Sericulture) ❑ B.V.Sc.(Bachelor of Veterinary Sciences) ❑ B.F.Sc.(Bachelor of Fisheries Sciences)	

Track: Commerce

Degree	Profession
❑ B.Com. ❑ B.Sc. (Accounting & Finance) ❑ BBA(Finance) ❑ BFA (Financial Accounting) ❑ B.Com. (Professional)	Accountant, Actuary / Actuarial science, Auditor, Banker, Certified Finance Analyst, Certified Financial Planner, Certified Investment Analyst, Certified Investment Banker, Certified Stock Broker, Chartered Accountant, Company Secretary, Cost and Works Accountant, Economist, Finance Analyst, Finance Consultant, Finance Controller, Finance Manager, Finance Planner,

	Investment Analyst, Portfolio Manager, Statistician, Stock Broker, Tax Auditor, Tax Consultant, Business Analyst

Higher Certification in Commerce:

Degree	**Institutions**
❑ CA (Chartered Accountant)	www.icai.org
❑ CS (Company Secretary)	www.icsi.edu
❑ CWA (Cost and Works Accountant)	www.icwai.org
❑ CFA (Certified Finance Analyst)	www.cfainstitute.org www.cfp.net
❑ CFP (Certified Financial Planner)	Various Private Institutions
❑ CIB (Certified Investment Banker)	www.nism.ac.in www.nism.ac.in
❑ CSB (Certified Stock Broker)	www.actuariesindia.org
❑ CIA (Certified Investment Analyst)	www.nseindia.com www.bsebti.com
❑ Certified Actuary	
❑ NSE & BSE Certifications	

Track: Arts / Humanities

Degree	Profession
❏ BA (Bachelor in Arts)	Anthropologist, Archaeologist, Curator, Economist, Editor, Geographer, Historian, Journalist, Language Trainer, Philosopher, Political Scientist, Psychologist, Restorer, Social Worker, Sociologist, Teacher, Translator, Writer

Specialisations in Bachelor of Arts:

- Psychology
- Economics
- Geography
- Journalism
- Philosophy
- Political Science
- Social Work
- Sociology
- Archaeology
- Museology
- Public Administration
- Indian / Foreign Language
- History
- Anthropology

Track: Law

Degree	Profession
❑ B.Sc. LLB (Bachelor in Science & Bachelor in Law) ❑ BA LLB (Bachelor in Arts & Bachelor in Law) ❑ B.Com. LLB (Bachelor in Commerce & Bachelor in Law) ❑ BBA LLB (Bachelor in Business Admin. & Bachelor in Law) ❑ BLS LLB (Bachelor in Liberal Arts & Bachelor in Law) ❑ BSW LLB (Bachelor in Social Work & Bachelor in Law) ❑ B.Tech. LLB (Bachelor in Technology & Bachelor in Law)	Litigator, Lawyer, Advocate, Social Activist, Diplomat, Judicial Magistrate, Judge, Professor, Legal Advisor, Corporate Legal Consultant, Arbitrator, Conciliator, Mediator etc.,

Track: Business Management

Degree	Profession
❑ BBA (Bachelor in Business Administration) ❑ BMS (Bachelor in Management Studies) ❑ BBS (Bachelor in Business Studies) ❑ BBM (Bachelor in Business Management) ❑ BBA+MBA Integrated Programme in Management	Executive, Manager, Administrator, Head or Consultant in the fields of Marketing/ HR/ Finance/ Systems & Operations/IT, Entrepreneur, Family Business Owner etc., Event Manager, Party Organizer, Wedding Planner, Business Analyst

Track: Hotel Management

Degree	Profession
❑ B.Sc. (Hospitality & Hotel Administration) ❑ BA (Hons.) in Hotel Management ❑ BA (Hons.) in Culinary Arts ❑ B.Tech. (Hotel Management and Catering Technology)	Caterer, Hotelier, Chef, Travel Manager, F&B Manager, Housekeeping Manager, Front Office Manager, Sales & Marketing Manager, Air Crew, Ship Crew, Restaurateur

Track: Liberal Studies

Degree	Profession
❏ BA (Hons.) with Diploma in Liberal Arts ❏ BBA (Hons.) with Diploma in Liberal Arts ❏ BCom. (Hons.) with Diploma in Liberal Arts ❏ BSc. (Hons.) with Diploma in Liberal Arts	Refer Arts/ Commerce/ Science or any other specialization which you major in.

Track: Mass Communication

Degree	Profession
❏ B.Sc. (Visual Communication) ❏ BMC (Bachelor in Mass Communication) ❏ BMS (Bachelor in Media Studies) ❏ BJMC (Bachelor in Journalism & Mass Communication) ❏ BA in Journalism/ Communication & Media	Anchor, Reporter, Journalist, Correspondent, Editor, Copywriter, Content Writer, Creative Writer, Director, Cinematographer, Media Programmer, Public Relations Specialist

Track: Economics

Degree	Profession
❑ BA (Hons.) Economics ❑ B.Sc. (Hons.) Economics	Economist, Financial Risk/Investment/Market Research/ Actuarial/ Data Analyst, Economic Journalist, Statistician etc.,

Track: Social Works

Degree	Profession
❑ BSW (Bachelor in Social Work) ❑ BA (Social Work) ❑ BSW+MSW (Bachelor + Master in Social Work) ❑ BRS (Bachelor in Rural studies)	Social Activist, Social Worker, Rural Development Officer, Volunteer with an NGO, Community Worker, Politician, Child and Women Welfare Worker etc.,

Track: Science / Computer Applications

Degree	Profession
❑ BCA (Bachelor in Computer Applications) ❑ BCA+MCA (Bachelor and Master in Computer Applications) ❑ B.Sc. Computer Science ❑ B.Sc. Maths ❑ B.Sc. Chemistry ❑ B.Sc. Statistics ❑ B.Sc. Physics ❑ BS-MS Integrated (Bachelor of Science - Master of Science Integrated) ❑ BBA-IT (Bachelor of Business Administration (Info.Tech.)	Actor or Actress, Dancer, Choreographer, Composer, Director, Programmer, IT Manager, System Engineer, Network/Software Engineer, Ethical Hacker, Animator, Game/ Web/ Application Designer, Mathematician, Scientist, Commercial Pilot, Astronaut, Naval Officer, Physicist, Statistician, Automobile Designer, Chemist etc.,

Track: Performing Arts

Degree	Profession
❑ BPA (Bachelor in Performing Arts) - Music, Acting, Singing	Actor or Actress, Dancer, Choreographer, Composer, Director, Dramatist, Musician, Performer, Screenwriter, Singer, Talent Manager, Theatre Artist, Trainer/Teacher, Vocalist

Track: Design / Fine Arts / Visual Arts

Degree	Profession
❑ B. Des. (Bachelor in Design) ❑ BFA (Bachelor in Fine Arts) ❑ BVA (Bachelor in Visual Arts) ❑ B.Cr.A(Bachelor in Creative Arts)	Apparel, Automobile, Ceramic, Exhibition, Fashion, Furniture, Game, Graphic, Industrial, Interior, Life Style, Accessory, Photography, Product, Textile, Toy Designer etc.,

Track: Sports

Degree	Profession
❑ BBA (Sports Management) ❑ BA (Sports Management) ❑ BPE (Bachelor in Physical Education)	Sports Manager, Player, Coach, Physical Trainer, Teacher, Athlete, Announcer, Commentator, Sports Analyst, Equipment Manager, Referee etc.

Track: Defense Sector

India's defense sector offers a wide range of career opportunities across its three primary branches—Indian Army, Indian Navy, and Indian Air Force—as well as paramilitary forces, defense research organizations, and technical services.

1. Indian Army Careers

- **Combat Roles**: Infantry, Armored Corps, Artillery, Engineers.
- **Technical Roles**: Corps of Signals, Electronics and Mechanical Engineers (EME), Army Aviation.
- **Support Services**: Army Medical Corps, Army Dental Corps, Army Education Corps.
- **Administrative Roles**: Judge Advocate General (JAG), Logistics and Supply Chain Management.
- **Special Forces**: Parachute Regiment (Para Commandos), National Security Guard (NSG).
- **Nursing and Healthcare**: Military Nursing Service (MNS).

2. Indian Navy Careers

- **Executive Branch**: General Service, Hydrography, Navigation, Aviation, Submariners, Law Officers.
- **Technical Branch**: Engineering, Electrical, Naval Architecture.
- **Medical Branch**: Doctors, Nurses, and Medical Specialists.
- **Submarine Service**: Specialist submarine operations.
- **Aviation Branch**: Pilots (fighter, transport, reconnaissance), Air Traffic Controllers.
- **Logistics and Administrative Roles**: Supply Chain Management, Legal, and Personnel Management.

- **Special Forces**: Marine Commandos (MARCOS).

3. Indian Air Force Careers

- **Flying Branch**: Fighter Pilots, Transport Pilots, Helicopter Pilots.
- **Technical Branch**: Aeronautical Engineering (Mechanical/Electronics).
- **Ground Duty (Non-Technical)**: Administration, Accounts, Logistics, Meteorology, Education.
- **Special Forces**: Garud Commando Force.

4. Paramilitary Forces

- **Border Security Force (BSF)**: Border management, counter-insurgency.
- **Central Reserve Police Force (CRPF)**: Internal security, disaster response.
- **Indo-Tibetan Border Police (ITBP)**: Guarding borders in mountainous regions.
- **Sashastra Seema Bal (SSB)**: Ensuring security on borders with Nepal and Bhutan.
- **Assam Rifles**: Counter-insurgency in the Northeast.
- **Central Industrial Security Force (CISF)**: Industrial security, airport security.

5. Research & Technical Roles

- **Defense Research and Development Organization (DRDO)**: Scientists, Engineers in various disciplines.

- **Ordnance Factories**: Manufacturing of weapons, ammunition.
- **Aeronautical Development Agency (ADA)**: Aircraft design and development.

6. Special Career Tracks

- **National Cadet Corps (NCC)**: Leading to direct entry in defense services.
- **Territorial Army**: Part-time military service.
- **Short Service Commission (SSC)**: Limited-period service in Army, Navy, or Air Force.

7. Intelligence and Cybersecurity

- **Intelligence Bureau (IB)**: Intelligence gathering, analysis.
- **Defense Intelligence Agency (DIA)**: Military intelligence.
- **National Technical Research Organization (NTRO)**: Cyber and satellite intelligence.
- **Cybersecurity Experts**: Protecting digital assets of defense organizations.

8. Defense Academies & Entry Modes

- **National Defence Academy (NDA)**: Entry after Class 12.
- **Indian Military Academy (IMA)**: Direct entry for graduates.
- **Air Force Academy (AFA)**: Pilots, technical officers.
- **Naval Academy (INA)**: Specialized Navy roles.
- **Officer Training Academy (OTA)**: SSC officers.
- **University Entry Scheme (UES)**: Engineering students.

9. Women in Defense

Women can pursue careers in:

- Flying roles (Air Force and Navy).
- Combat roles (Army Corps of Engineers, Navy).
- Technical and medical branches.
- Special entry schemes like Women Entry Scheme and MNS.

10. Other Opportunities

- **Defense Journalism**: Reporting on military events.
- **Defense Consultants**: Strategic planning and analysis.
- **Private Defense Companies**: Working with organizations like HAL, BEL, or private defense contractors.

Each role requires specific eligibility criteria, educational qualifications, and physical standards. Aspirants can choose their career based on interest, qualifications, and dedication to serving the nation.

Track: Civil Services

In India, the Civil Services comprises various streams and services, including but not limited to the following:

All India Services

1. **Indian Administrative Service (IAS)**: Responsible for administrative functions, policy formulation, and implementation at the central and state levels.
2. **Indian Police Service (IPS)**: Manages public order, crime prevention, and law enforcement across the country.
3. **Indian Forest Service (IFS)**: Focuses on forest conservation, wildlife protection, and environmental policy.

Central Civil Services – Group A

1. **Indian Foreign Service (IFS)**: Represents India in foreign relations, diplomacy, and international affairs.
2. **Indian Revenue Service (IRS)**:
    - **IRS (Income Tax)**: Administers income tax laws and policies, revenue collection.
    - **IRS (Customs and Central Excise)**: Handles customs duties, GST, and other indirect taxes.
3. **Indian Audit and Accounts Service (IA&AS)**: Conducts audits for the Government of India and manages public funds.
4. **Indian Information Service (IIS)**: Deals with public communication, media, and information dissemination for the government.
5. **Indian Trade Service (ITS)**: Focuses on trade policies, export promotion, and trade regulations.
6. **Indian Civil Accounts Service (ICAS)**: Manages the financial accounts of the Government of India.
7. **Indian Defence Accounts Service (IDAS)**: Oversees financial management for the armed forces.

8. **Indian Ordnance Factories Service (IOFS)**: Manages India's ordnance factories and related defense production units.
9. **Indian Postal Service (IPoS)**: Administers postal services and related operations.
10. **Railway Services**: Manages the Indian Railways' various operations, including accounts, traffic, and engineering.

Central Civil Services – Group B

1. **Central Secretariat Services (CSS)**: Assists in administrative and policy-related work in central ministries and departments.
2. **Armed Forces Headquarters Civil Services (AFHQCS)**: Provides administrative support to the Ministry of Defence and armed forces.

Specialized Services

- **Indian Corporate Law Service (ICLS)**: Focuses on corporate law, governance, and compliance.
- **Indian Statistical Service (ISS)**: Involves statistical analysis and implementation of data-driven policies.
- **Indian Economic Service (IES)**: Deals with economic planning, policy-making, and analysis.

These services are primarily recruited through the **Union Public Service Commission (UPSC)** Civil Services Examination and other specialized exams.

Chapter 7: Behavioural / Soft Skills

Developing Behavioural skills / Power Skills during early days is essential for personal growth, building relationships, and preparing for future challenges. Behavioural skills develop over time and improve as they are incorporated into daily life. Here are key behavioural skills students should focus on. Start small and practice consistently with some of the techniques listed below.

Personal Development Skills		
Skill	**Description**	**Techniques**
Self-discipline	Managing time and responsibilities effectively Completing tasks without postponement	• Create a <u>daily schedule</u> and stick to it. • <u>Break tasks</u> into smaller steps and prioritize them. • Use timers or apps to focus on tasks (e.g., Pomodoro technique). • <u>Reward yourself</u> for completing goals.
Emotional Regulation	Understanding and managing emotions to stay calm and focused under pressure	• Practice <u>deep breathing</u> or mindfulness when stressed. • Keep a journal to express feelings and identify triggers. • <u>Learn to pause and think before reacting</u> in emotional situations.
Resilience	Learning to cope with setbacks Adapting to changes, and staying determined	• <u>Reframe challenges as opportunities</u> to learn. • <u>Surround yourself with supportive friends</u> and mentors. • <u>Celebrate small wins</u> and progress regularly.
Confidence	Believing in one's abilities and expressing oneself clearly	• <u>Practice public speaking</u> or participate in debates. • <u>Set small, achievable goals</u> to build a sense of accomplishment. • <u>Focus on strengths</u> and positive affirmations.

Interpersonal Skills		
Skill	**Description**	**Techniques**
Empathy	Understanding and respecting the feelings of others	• Actively listen without interrupting. • Volunteer for community service to understand others' perspectives. • Ask questions to learn how others feel or think.
Communication	Developing both verbal and non-verbal skills to express ideas clearly and listen actively	• Engage in discussions and ask questions in class. • Practice writing clearly and concisely (e.g., letters, essays). • Maintain eye contact and positive body language when speaking.
Teamwork	Working collaboratively with peers and contributing effectively to group projects	• Join group activities like sports, clubs, or projects. • Share responsibilities equally and appreciate others' contributions. • Practice resolving disagreements collaboratively.
Conflict resolution	Handling disagreements constructively and finding solutions amicably	• Stay calm and focus on the issue, not the person. • Use "I" statements (e.g., "I feel…" instead of "You always…"). • Seek compromise or mediation if needed.

<table>
<tr><th colspan="3" align="center">Social and Ethical Skills</th></tr>
<tr><th align="center">Skill</th><th align="center">Description</th><th align="center">Techniques</th></tr>
<tr>
<td>Respect</td>
<td>Treating others with kindness and valuing diverse opinions and backgrounds.</td>
<td>

- Practice active listening without interrupting.
- Be inclusive and considerate in group settings.
- Show gratitude by saying "thank you" and "please."

</td>
</tr>
<tr>
<td>Accountability</td>
<td>Taking responsibility for one's actions and accepting consequences</td>
<td>

- Admit mistakes and learn from them.
- Keep promises and commitments.
- Use tools like planners to track responsibilities.

</td>
</tr>
<tr>
<td>Integrity</td>
<td>Being honest, ethical, and consistent in actions</td>
<td>

- Be truthful in exams, projects, and interactions.
- Reflect on your values and align your actions accordingly.

</td>
</tr>
<tr>
<td>Manners and etiquette</td>
<td>Using polite language, showing gratitude, and following social norms</td>
<td>

- Learn basic etiquette (e.g., greeting elders, table manners).
- Show appreciation through thank-you notes or gestures.
- Practice patience and kindness in social settings.

</td>
</tr>
</table>

<table>
<tr><th colspan="3">Cognitive and Learning Skills</th></tr>
<tr><th>Skill</th><th>Description</th><th>Techniques</th></tr>
<tr>
<td>Critical Thinking</td>
<td>Analysing situations and solving problems logically</td>
<td>

- Ask "why" and "how" to understand topics deeply.
- Solve puzzles, play strategy games, or engage in logic-based activities.
- Practice analysing pros and cons before making decisions.

</td>
</tr>
<tr>
<td>Curiosity</td>
<td>Asking questions and seeking knowledge proactively</td>
<td>

- Read books, watch documentaries, or explore hobbies.
- Join interest-based clubs or forums to discuss ideas.
- Take on personal projects to explore new areas.

</td>
</tr>
<tr>
<td>Adaptability</td>
<td>Being open to learning new concepts and adjusting to various environments</td>
<td>

- Try new experiences (e.g., learning a language or skill).
- Accept feedback constructively and use it to improve.
- Focus on solutions rather than dwelling on problems.

</td>
</tr>
<tr>
<td>Focus & Attention</td>
<td>Maintaining concentration during classes and activities</td>
<td>

- Use meditation or exercises to improve concentration.
- Minimize distractions by organizing your workspace.
- Practice active listening

</td>
</tr>
</table>

Leadership and Initiative		
Skill	**Description**	**Techniques**
Decision Making	Weighing options carefully before choosing a course of action	• <u>List out options</u> and evaluate their outcomes. • <u>Start by making small decisions</u> to build confidence. • <u>Reflect on past decisions</u> to identify improvements.
Motivation	Staying enthusiastic about learning and achieving goals	• <u>Set clear, specific goals</u> and visualize their benefits. • <u>Reward yourself</u> for progress, not just results. • <u>Surround yourself with positive role models.</u>
Influence	Inspiring and positively impacting peers and the community	• <u>Share ideas confidently</u> and back them with logic. • Support and mentor peers in their tasks. • <u>Participate in leadership roles</u> in clubs or teams.
Responsibility	Leading by example and managing assigned roles diligently	• <u>Take ownership</u> of class assignments and deadlines. • <u>Offer to lead small projects</u> or organize events. • Learn from mistakes and focus on improvement.

Conclusion

As we draw to the conclusion of Discover You, this book serves as more than just a guide—it is a companion in the transformative journey of career discovery and decision-making. By combining the wisdom of traditional career counseling with the cutting-edge power of Artificial Intelligence, we have opened the doors to over **90 diverse career paths** and unlocked **insights into 900+ companies, Institutes and Organizations.** Each chapter aims to inspire clarity, confidence, and ambition in students, parents, and educators.

The **AI-enabled career videos** provide a dynamic window into professions, demystifying complex roles and empowering informed choices. Meanwhile, the comprehensive **list of career journey tracks** ensures that every reader has a clear and actionable roadmap tailored to their unique interests and potential.

How to use AI prompts help users simulate real-world scenarios, explore potential career paths, and even discover unconventional opportunities that align with their passions and abilities. The book also provides detailed **insights into various emerging careers in AI.**

Discover You is not just a book but a movement—a call to embrace curiosity, harness innovation, and reimagine the future of education and careers. For students, it is a compass pointing towards meaningful opportunities. For parents, it offers the reassurance of informed guidance. And for educators, it is a tool to nurture and shape the leaders of tomorrow.

Let this guide be the spark that ignites your journey toward fulfillment, success, and purpose. Remember, discovering yourself is the first step to transforming the world around you.

Your future awaits - Go out Discover You!